LanGraph

A Hands-On Guide to Building and Scaling Autonomous Multi-Agent Systems

Written By

Maxime lane

LangGraph in Action: A Hands-On Guide to Building and Scaling Autonomous Multi-Agent Systems

Table of Contents

Preface 4

Chapter 1: Overview of LangGraph and Autonomous Systems 9

Chapter 2: Getting Started with LangGraph 28

Chapter 3: Fundamentals of Autonomous Multi-Agent Systems 40

Chapter 4: Graph Theory Essentials for LangGraph 57

Chapter 5: Inside the LangGraph Architecture 75

Chapter 6: Designing Your Multi-Agent System.....................................92

Chapter 7: Implementing Autonomous Agents in LangGraph 109

Chapter 8: Advanced LangGraph Techniques and Patterns...................128

Chapter 9: Principles of Scalability in Multi-Agent Systems..................142

Chapter 10: Performance Optimization Techniques..............................155

Chapter 12: Practical Applications of LangGraph.................................187

Chapter 13: Troubleshooting and Maintenance 209

Chapter 14: Future Trends and Innovations 228

Chapter 15: Appendices and Resources...245

Index..260

Conclusion..269

Preface

Welcome to **"LanGraph: A Hands-On Guide to Building and Scaling Autonomous Multi-Agent Systems."** This preface lays the groundwork for what you can expect from this book. Whether you are a developer looking to expand your technical toolkit or a system architect aiming to implement robust, scalable solutions, this guide is designed to be your practical companion throughout the journey.

Purpose of the Book

The primary goal of this book is to serve as a comprehensive, hands-on guide that equips you with the knowledge and tools necessary to build and scale autonomous multi-agent systems using LangGraph. In today's fast-evolving technological landscape, systems that can operate autonomously, adapt to changes, and work together seamlessly are in high demand. This guide covers:

- **Conceptual Foundations:** We begin with the basics of LangGraph and the principles behind autonomous multi-agent systems, ensuring you understand the theory as well as the practice.
- **Practical Implementation:** Through clear, step-by-step tutorials and code examples, you will learn how to develop agents, manage their interactions, and integrate them into larger systems.
- **Scalability and Optimization:** As systems grow in complexity, performance and scalability become critical. Detailed chapters address how to optimize communication, manage resources, and deploy systems in distributed environments.
- **Real-World Applications:** The guide is enriched with case studies and examples from various industries such as robotics, finance, IoT, and more, demonstrating the versatility and power of LangGraph.

This book is designed to be both an educational resource and a practical reference, bridging the gap between theory and practice in a clear, accessible manner.

Who Should Read This Book

This book is tailored for a diverse audience, including but not limited to:

- **Software Developers and Engineers:** Those looking to expand their expertise into autonomous systems and distributed architectures.
- **System Architects:** Professionals who design complex systems and need robust strategies for scalability and performance.
- **Researchers and Academics:** Individuals interested in the theoretical underpinnings of graph-based models and their practical applications.
- **Tech Enthusiasts:** Anyone with a passion for modern technologies, who wants to understand how autonomous multi-agent systems work in real-world scenarios.

Prerequisites:
A basic understanding of programming concepts is recommended. Familiarity with any high-level programming language (such as Python, Java, or C++) will be helpful when working through the code examples and exercises. No prior experience with LangGraph or multi-agent systems is required, as this guide starts from the fundamentals and builds up to more advanced topics.

How to Use This Book

This book is organized into multiple parts that progressively build your knowledge and skills:

1. **Foundational Concepts:**
   The first sections introduce LangGraph, the principles of autonomous multi-agent systems, and the relevant aspects of graph theory. This part sets the stage for understanding the deeper technical content that follows.
2. **Hands-On Development:**
   Detailed chapters provide step-by-step instructions on building your own autonomous agents and integrating them using LangGraph. Code examples, exercises, and real-world scenarios help reinforce the concepts covered.
3. **Advanced Techniques and Scaling:**
   Later sections focus on optimizing performance, scaling systems for

high availability, and deploying them in cloud or distributed environments. These chapters are packed with practical advice and best practices.

4. **Case Studies and Future Trends:**
   Real-world applications and case studies illustrate how these systems are implemented in various industries. Additionally, discussions on emerging trends and future innovations provide insights into where the technology is headed.

5. **Companion Materials:**
   To complement the content in the book, you will find online repositories, supplementary tutorials, and additional reading materials. These resources are designed to help you experiment with code, view interactive diagrams, and further solidify your understanding.

Throughout the book, each chapter is structured to build on previous lessons. Diagrams, tables, and code snippets are used to make complex ideas easier to grasp. At the end of each section, review questions and practical exercises allow you to test your understanding and apply what you've learned.

Conventions and Notations

To ensure clarity and consistency throughout the book, we adhere to the following conventions and notations:

Code Style

- **Syntax Highlighting:**
  Code examples are presented in a monospaced font with syntax highlighting to distinguish between keywords, variables, and comments. For instance, a Python example might look like this:

python

```
def hello_world():
    # This function prints 'Hello, World!'
    print("Hello, World!")

if __name__ == "__main__":
    hello_world()
```

- **Commenting:**
  Comments are used liberally to explain what each section of the code does, ensuring that even readers new to the language can follow along.

Diagrams and Flowcharts

- **Clarity in Visuals:**
  Diagrams and flowcharts are designed to be simple and clear, with consistent symbols and labels. For example, nodes in a graph diagram represent agents, while arrows indicate communication or data flow.
- **Legend and Keys:**
  Each diagram includes a legend or key where necessary, so that readers can easily understand the symbols and their meanings.

Tables

Tables are used to summarize key concepts, compare different approaches, or list important commands and settings. Here is an example of a simple table used in the book:

Element	Notation/Example	Description
Code Block	python def hello_world(): print("Hello, World!")	A basic code block in Python.
Graph Node	●	Represents an autonomous agent in a system.
Communication Arrow	→	Indicates data flow or message passing between agents.

General Notations

- **Bold Text:**
  Used for key terms and definitions to make them stand out.
- **Italics:**
  Employed for emphasis or to denote technical terms upon first introduction.

- **Headings and Subheadings:**
  The book is divided into clearly labeled sections, chapters, and subchapters, which help guide the reader through the material logically.

These conventions have been chosen to make the material accessible, especially for those who are new to the subject, while still providing the detail needed by more advanced readers.

Acknowledgments

This book is the result of a collaborative effort, and it would not have been possible without the support, expertise, and encouragement of many individuals and communities. I would like to extend my deepest gratitude to:

- **The LangGraph Community:**
  For sharing insights, providing valuable feedback, and fostering an environment of innovation.
- **Subject Matter Experts:**
  Whose contributions and peer reviews have helped refine the technical content of this book.
- **Developers and Practitioners:**
  Who shared real-world experiences and case studies that enriched the practical aspects of the guide.
- **Editors and Proofreaders:**
  For ensuring that the language is clear, the examples are accurate, and the overall presentation is professional.
- **Family and Friends:**
  For their unwavering support and encouragement throughout the writing process.

Their contributions, big and small, have been instrumental in creating a resource that aims to empower you with the skills and knowledge to succeed in building advanced autonomous multi-agent systems.

Thank you for choosing this book. I hope it becomes a valuable resource in your journey toward mastering LangGraph and designing the next generation of autonomous systems. Let's embark on this exciting journey together!

Chapter 1: Overview of LangGraph and Autonomous Systems

In this chapter, we will introduce LangGraph—what it is, why it matters, and how it serves as a powerful framework for building autonomous multi-agent systems. We will also explore the evolution of autonomous systems, tracing their historical context, technological milestones, current trends, and future prospects.

1.1 What is LangGraph?

Introduction to LangGraph as a Framework

LangGraph is a versatile and robust framework designed to simplify the development and management of autonomous multi-agent systems. At its core, LangGraph leverages graph theory principles to model, visualize, and manage the interactions between multiple autonomous agents. In a LangGraph system, each agent is represented as a node in a graph, while the communication or relationships between these agents are depicted as edges. This graph-based approach allows for a clear, modular, and scalable way to design complex systems.

By abstracting agents and their interactions into graph components, LangGraph enables developers to:

- **Visualize System Dynamics:** Easily see how agents connect and interact.
- **Modularize Code:** Organize agents and their behaviors into discrete, manageable modules.
- **Scale Easily:** Add or remove agents without disrupting the overall system structure.
- **Enhance Debugging and Maintenance:** Isolate issues through clear graph relationships and modular design.

Key Features and Benefits

Below is a table summarizing the key features and benefits of LangGraph:

Feature	Description	Benefit
Graph-Based Architecture	Models agents as nodes and interactions as edges, leveraging proven graph theory principles.	Simplifies visualization and management of complex systems.
Modular Design	Encourages encapsulation of agent logic into discrete modules.	Eases development, testing, and maintenance.
Scalability	Supports adding or removing agents dynamically, ensuring system resilience as it grows.	Facilitates building large-scale autonomous systems.
Robust Communication	Provides built-in support for various communication protocols among agents.	Enhances reliability and efficiency in agent interactions.
Extensibility	Designed to integrate with third-party APIs, machine learning models, and external data sources.	Offers flexibility to adapt to diverse application needs.
Real-Time Monitoring	Comes with tools to monitor agent performance and visualize the system in real time.	Assists in troubleshooting and performance optimization.

A Simple Code Example

To illustrate how LangGraph works in practice, consider the following basic Python code snippet. This example demonstrates how to create a simple agent, add it to a LangGraph system, and simulate communication between agents.

python

```python
# Importing the hypothetical LangGraph framework components
from langgraph import Agent, GraphSystem

# Define a simple autonomous agent class by inheriting from Agent
class HelloAgent(Agent):
    def __init__(self, name):
        super().__init__(name)
```

```python
    def act(self, message):
        """
        This method defines the agent's action upon receiving a message.
        For simplicity, it just prints out the message.
        """
        print(f"{self.name} received: {message}")

# Create an instance of the LangGraph system
system = GraphSystem()

# Instantiate two agents with distinct names
agent_A = HelloAgent("Agent A")
agent_B = HelloAgent("Agent B")

# Add the agents to the LangGraph system
system.add_agent(agent_A)
system.add_agent(agent_B)

# Simulate communication: Agent A sends a message to Agent B
agent_A.send("Hello from Agent A", target=agent_B)
```

Explanation of the Code:

- **Importing Components:**
  The code begins by importing Agent and GraphSystem from the LangGraph framework.
- **Defining an Agent:**
  A new class HelloAgent is defined, inheriting from the Agent base class. The act method is overridden to specify what the agent does when it receives a message.
- **Setting Up the System:**
  An instance of GraphSystem is created. Two agents, agent_A and agent_B, are instantiated and added to this system.
- **Simulating Communication:**
  Finally, agent_A sends a message to agent_B. When agent_B receives the message, it executes its act method, printing out the received message.

This simple example demonstrates how LangGraph abstracts agent communication, making it straightforward to set up and manage interactions within a multi-agent system.

1.2 The Evolution of Autonomous Multi-Agent Systems

Historical Context and Technological Milestones

The development of autonomous multi-agent systems has evolved significantly over the decades. Understanding this evolution provides context for the innovations embedded in frameworks like LangGraph.

Early Developments

- **Foundational Theories (1940s-1960s):**
  The conceptual underpinnings of autonomous systems can be traced back to early work in cybernetics and control theory. Pioneers such as Norbert Wiener and Alan Turing laid the groundwork for understanding machine intelligence and feedback systems.
- **Early Robotics (1970s-1980s):**
  With the advent of programmable robots, researchers began experimenting with machines capable of basic autonomous behaviors. The focus during this era was largely on individual robotic agents performing specific tasks in controlled environments.

Advancements in Multi-Agent Systems

- **Emergence of Distributed AI (1990s):**
  The 1990s saw a shift from isolated robotic agents to systems where multiple agents could interact and cooperate. This period marked the birth of multi-agent system research, emphasizing collaboration, communication, and distributed decision-making.
- **Technological Milestones:**
  - **Agent Communication Languages:**
    Standardized languages such as KQML (Knowledge Query and Manipulation Language) and FIPA (Foundation for Intelligent Physical Agents) protocols were developed to facilitate agent interactions.
  - **Simulation Platforms:**
    Tools and frameworks began emerging to simulate multi-agent environments, enabling researchers to test and refine agent behaviors in virtual settings.

A Timeline of Key Milestones

Below is a timeline that captures some of the significant milestones in the evolution of autonomous multi-agent systems:

Era	Milestone	Impact
1940s-1960s	Early cybernetics and control theory	Laid the theoretical foundation for machine autonomy.
1970s-1980s	Development of programmable robots	Demonstrated the feasibility of autonomous behavior.
1990s	Emergence of distributed AI and multi-agent system research	Enabled cooperation and communication among agents.
Late 1990s-2000s	Introduction of agent communication languages (KQML, FIPA)	Standardized interactions in multi-agent systems.
2000s-Present	Advancements in real-time processing, IoT, and machine learning	Led to highly dynamic, scalable, and intelligent systems.

Current Trends and Future Prospects

Current Trends

Today, autonomous multi-agent systems are at the forefront of technological innovation. Some of the key trends include:

- **Integration with Artificial Intelligence:**
  Modern multi-agent systems increasingly incorporate AI and machine learning techniques to improve decision-making, predict behaviors, and adapt to new situations. These systems are capable of learning from interactions and optimizing their performance over time.
- **Internet of Things (IoT) and Edge Computing:**
  With the explosion of IoT devices, multi-agent systems are now being deployed in environments where agents communicate across distributed networks, often at the edge. This enhances responsiveness and reduces reliance on centralized data centers.

- **Decentralized Architectures:**
  The push towards decentralization has spurred the development of frameworks that allow agents to operate independently while still coordinating effectively. This trend is particularly evident in blockchain-based systems and distributed ledgers.

Future Prospects

Looking forward, the field of autonomous multi-agent systems promises even more exciting developments:

- **Enhanced Autonomy and Adaptability:**
  Future systems will likely be more autonomous, capable of complex decision-making without human intervention. This will be driven by advances in AI, deep learning, and real-time data analytics.
- **Increased Collaboration Across Domains:**
  As the boundaries between different technological domains blur, we can expect more integrated systems that combine robotics, IoT, cloud computing, and AI. LangGraph and similar frameworks will play a crucial role in enabling this convergence.
- **Ethical and Regulatory Considerations:**
  As autonomous systems become more prevalent, ensuring ethical deployment and adherence to regulations will be critical. Researchers and practitioners will need to address issues such as accountability, transparency, and data privacy.
- **Innovative Applications:**
  From smart cities and autonomous transportation to personalized healthcare and adaptive manufacturing, the applications for autonomous multi-agent systems are vast. Ongoing research and development will continue to unlock new possibilities and redefine how we interact with technology.

By understanding both what LangGraph offers as a framework and the historical evolution of autonomous multi-agent systems, you are now better equipped to appreciate the context and capabilities of the technologies discussed in this book. In the chapters that follow, we will build upon these foundational concepts, providing hands-on examples and practical guidance to help you harness the power of LangGraph in your own projects.

1.3 The Role of Graph Theory in Modern System Design

Graph theory is a branch of mathematics that studies graphs—mathematical structures used to model pairwise relations between objects. In modern system design, particularly in the development of autonomous multi-agent systems, graph theory provides a natural and powerful framework for modeling complex interactions. This section explores the basics of graph theory and explains why graphs are an ideal model for representing agent interactions.

Basics of Graph Theory

At its core, a **graph** is a collection of objects, called **vertices** (or **nodes**), and the connections between them, known as **edges**. Graphs can be used to represent various systems where entities interact with one another.

Key Definitions

- **Vertex (Node):**
  A fundamental unit in a graph that represents an entity. In the context of autonomous systems, each vertex can represent an individual agent.
- **Edge:**
  A connection between two vertices that represents a relationship or interaction. In agent systems, an edge might denote communication or data exchange between agents.
- **Directed Graph:**
  A graph where edges have a direction, indicating a one-way relationship. For example, if Agent A sends data to Agent B, the edge from A to B is directed.
- **Undirected Graph:**
  A graph where edges do not have a direction, meaning the relationship is mutual. This is useful in systems where interactions are bidirectional.
- **Weighted Graph:**
  A graph where each edge has a numerical value (weight) associated with it. Weights can represent the cost, strength, or capacity of the connection between agents.

Summary Table of Graph Terms

Term	Definition	Example in Agent Systems
Vertex (Node)	An individual entity within a graph.	A single autonomous agent.
Edge	A connection or relationship between two vertices.	Communication or data exchange between agents.
Directed Graph	A graph with edges that have a specific direction.	Agent A sending a command to Agent B.
Undirected Graph	A graph with edges that have no specific direction.	Peer-to-peer communication between agents.
Weighted Graph	A graph where edges have associated numerical values.	Network latency or bandwidth between agents.

A Simple Code Example Using Python's NetworkX

Below is a basic example demonstrating how to create and visualize a graph representing autonomous agents using the NetworkX library. This example shows three agents connected to each other.

python

```
import networkx as nx
import matplotlib.pyplot as plt

# Create an empty, undirected graph
G = nx.Graph()

# Add nodes representing autonomous agents
G.add_node("Agent A")
G.add_node("Agent B")
G.add_node("Agent C")

# Add edges representing the interactions (communication links) between
agents
G.add_edge("Agent A", "Agent B")
G.add_edge("Agent A", "Agent C")
G.add_edge("Agent B", "Agent C")

# Draw the graph with labels
```

```
nx.draw(G, with_labels=True, node_color='lightblue', edge_color='gray',
node_size=1500, font_size=12)
plt.title("Graph Representation of Autonomous Agents")
plt.show()
```

Explanation of the Code:

- **Importing Libraries:**
  The code begins by importing the networkx library for graph creation
  and matplotlib.pyplot for visualization.
- **Creating the Graph:**
  An undirected graph G is created using nx.Graph().
- **Adding Nodes:**
  Three nodes are added to the graph, each representing an autonomous
  agent.
- **Adding Edges:**
  Edges are added between the nodes to represent interactions (e.g.,
  communication channels) between agents.
- **Visualizing the Graph:**
  The nx.draw() function is used to draw the graph. Customizations
  such as node color, edge color, and font size help make the
  visualization clear.

Why Graphs Are an Ideal Model for Agent Interactions

Graphs naturally map to the structure of autonomous multi-agent systems for
several reasons:

1. **Clear Visualization of Interactions:**
   Graphs provide a visual representation of how agents interact. By
   representing agents as nodes and interactions as edges, it becomes
   easy to see the overall system architecture, identify clusters of agents,
   and pinpoint potential bottlenecks.
2. **Modularity and Scalability:**
   Since each agent is a node and each interaction an edge, adding or
   removing an agent from the system is straightforward. This
   modularity makes graphs an excellent tool for designing systems that
   can scale dynamically as agents are added or removed.
3. **Flexibility in Modeling Relationships:**
   Graphs can model various types of interactions—one-way, two-way,

or weighted by importance or cost. This flexibility is crucial when designing systems with complex communication protocols or prioritization strategies.

4. **Foundation for Advanced Algorithms:**
   Many algorithms in computer science, such as shortest path, clustering, and traversal algorithms, are based on graph theory. These algorithms can be directly applied to optimize communication, resource distribution, and overall system performance in a multi-agent system.

5. **Efficient Data Structures:**
   Graphs are supported by efficient data structures and libraries, making them ideal for handling large-scale systems with many agents and interactions. This efficiency is essential for real-time processing and decision-making.

1.4 Use Cases and Applications

Autonomous multi-agent systems built on frameworks like LangGraph have a wide range of applications across various industries. This section explores some of the industry-specific applications, highlighting how these systems are transforming traditional practices.

Industry-Specific Applications

Robotics

Application:

- **Swarm Robotics:** In swarm robotics, a group of robots operates autonomously and collaborates to achieve a common goal. Each robot (agent) communicates with others to navigate, avoid obstacles, and coordinate tasks.

Benefits:

- **Increased Efficiency:** Robots can cover large areas, work in parallel, and adapt to changing environments.
- **Enhanced Reliability:** The failure of one robot does not cripple the entire system, as other agents can compensate.

Example Scenario:
Imagine a fleet of drones used in agriculture to monitor crop health. Each drone gathers data and shares information with nearby drones to optimize flight paths and ensure complete coverage of the field.

Finance

Application:

- **Algorithmic Trading:** Autonomous agents can execute trades based on real-time market data. Each agent analyzes specific market signals and collaborates with others to adjust trading strategies.
- **Fraud Detection:** Agents monitor transactions across networks, detecting anomalics and alerting central systems to potential fraud.

Benefits:

- **Real-Time Decision Making:** Rapid processing of data enables timely execution of trades.
- **Enhanced Security:** Continuous monitoring across multiple nodes increases the chances of early fraud detection.

Example Scenario:
In an algorithmic trading system, each agent may be responsible for monitoring different market segments. They communicate significant market movements to a central system, which then rebalances the portfolio accordingly.

Internet of Things (IoT)

Application:

- **Smart Homes and Buildings:** Autonomous agents manage devices such as lights, thermostats, and security cameras. These systems learn from user behavior and optimize energy consumption.
- **Industrial IoT:** Sensors and machines on a factory floor communicate to monitor performance, predict maintenance needs, and optimize production processes.

Benefits:

- **Optimized Resource Usage:** Real-time data sharing allows for efficient energy and resource management.
- **Improved Safety and Maintenance:** Early detection of issues through continuous monitoring can prevent costly breakdowns.

Example Scenario:
In a smart building, autonomous agents adjust heating, ventilation, and air conditioning (HVAC) settings based on occupancy and weather forecasts, ensuring comfort while reducing energy costs.

Healthcare

Application:

- **Patient Monitoring:** Autonomous systems collect data from wearable devices and sensors to monitor patient health in real time.
- **Telemedicine:** Agents facilitate remote consultations by managing patient data and coordinating virtual appointments.

Benefits:

- **Timely Interventions:** Continuous monitoring enables early detection of health issues.
- **Personalized Care:** Data-driven insights help tailor treatments to individual patient needs.

Example Scenario:
In a hospital, a network of autonomous agents monitors patients in the intensive care unit (ICU). The agents alert medical staff immediately if a patient's vital signs deviate from the norm, enabling swift intervention.

Transportation

Application:

- **Traffic Management:** Autonomous systems manage traffic signals and optimize routing based on real-time data from various sensors and cameras.
- **Autonomous Vehicles:** Vehicles communicate with each other to navigate safely, share road condition information, and optimize travel routes.

Benefits:

- **Reduced Congestion:** Coordinated traffic management can significantly alleviate bottlenecks.
- **Enhanced Safety:** Continuous communication between vehicles helps prevent accidents.

Example Scenario:
In a smart city, autonomous traffic control agents adjust traffic lights based on real-time congestion data. This coordination minimizes delays and enhances the overall flow of traffic.

Summary Table of Use Cases

Industry	Application	Benefits
Robotics	Swarm robotics, collaborative drones	Increased efficiency, enhanced reliability
Finance	Algorithmic trading, fraud detection	Real-time decision making, enhanced security
IoT	Smart homes, industrial IoT sensors	Optimized resource usage, improved safety
Healthcare	Patient monitoring, telemedicine	Timely interventions, personalized care
Transportation	Traffic management, autonomous vehicles	Reduced congestion, enhanced safety

Graph theory not only provides the theoretical foundation for modeling complex relationships but also offers practical tools and algorithms that are essential in designing modern autonomous multi-agent systems. By representing agents as nodes and their interactions as edges, systems become easier to visualize, manage, and scale. This makes graph-based frameworks like LangGraph particularly powerful in diverse applications—from robotics and finance to IoT, healthcare, and transportation.

Understanding these concepts and real-world applications equips you with the insight needed to explore and implement advanced multi-agent systems. In the following chapters, we will delve deeper into the implementation details, offering hands-on tutorials and detailed examples to help you harness the full potential of LangGraph in your projects.

1.5 Book Structure and Roadmap

This section provides an overview of how the book is organized and what you can expect to learn from each section. By outlining the structure and learning objectives, we aim to give you a clear roadmap for your journey through LangGraph and autonomous multi-agent systems. Whether you are new to these topics or looking to deepen your understanding, this book is designed to guide you step by step through theory, practical implementation, and advanced optimization techniques.

How the Book is Organized

The book is divided into several distinct parts, each focused on a specific aspect of LangGraph and autonomous multi-agent systems. Here's a high-level overview of the structure:

Part	Title	Focus Areas
I	**Introduction to LangGraph and Autonomous Multi-Agent Systems**	Provides an overview of LangGraph, the evolution of autonomous systems, and the role of graph theory in modern design. Establishes the foundational context and introduces key concepts.
II	**Core Concepts and Fundamentals**	Covers the theoretical underpinnings of autonomous agents, core principles of graph theory, and an in-depth look at the architecture of LangGraph. Prepares you with the essential knowledge needed to build robust systems.

Part	Title	Focus Areas
III	**Building Autonomous Multi-Agent Systems with LangGraph**	Focuses on practical design and implementation. You will learn how to design, develop, and implement autonomous agents using hands-on tutorials, detailed code examples, and best practices for system development.
IV	**Scaling and Optimizing Your Systems**	Addresses the challenges of scalability and performance. This section includes strategies for performance optimization, resource management, and techniques for deploying systems in cloud or distributed environments.
V	**Real-World Applications and Future Directions**	Explores diverse industry applications such as robotics, finance, IoT, healthcare, and transportation. It also covers troubleshooting, maintenance, and emerging trends to help you stay ahead in this rapidly evolving field.
VI	**Appendices and Reference Materials**	Contains supplementary materials including installation guides, API references, a glossary of terms, further reading, and an index to help you quickly locate topics of interest.

Additional Visualization: JSON Representation

For those who appreciate a structured data view, here's a JSON representation of the book structure:

json

```
{
  "Part I": {
    "Title": "Introduction to LangGraph and Autonomous Multi-Agent
Systems",
    "Chapters": [
      "Overview of LangGraph and Autonomous Systems",
      "Getting Started with LangGraph"
    ]
  },
  "Part II": {
    "Title": "Core Concepts and Fundamentals",
```

```
  "Chapters": [
    "Fundamentals of Autonomous Multi-Agent Systems",
    "Graph Theory Essentials for LangGraph",
    "Inside the LangGraph Architecture"
  ]
},
"Part III": {
  "Title": "Building Autonomous Multi-Agent Systems with LangGraph",
  "Chapters": [
    "Designing Your Multi-Agent System",
    "Implementing Autonomous Agents in LangGraph",
    "Advanced LangGraph Techniques and Patterns"
  ]
},
"Part IV": {
  "Title": "Scaling and Optimizing Your Systems",
  "Chapters": [
    "Principles of Scalability in Multi-Agent Systems",
    "Performance Optimization Techniques",
    "Cloud Deployment and Distributed Architectures"
  ]
},
"Part V": {
  "Title": "Real-World Applications and Future Directions",
  "Chapters": [
    "Practical Applications of LangGraph",
    "Troubleshooting and Maintenance",
    "Future Trends and Innovations"
  ]
},
"Part VI": {
  "Title": "Appendices and Reference Materials",
  "Chapters": [
    "Appendices and Resources"
  ]
}
}
```

Explanation:

- Each part is clearly defined by its focus area, ensuring a logical progression from basic concepts to advanced applications.

- The JSON structure provides a programmatically friendly view of the content organization, which may be particularly useful if you are planning to integrate these resources into a digital learning platform.

What You Can Expect to Learn

This book is designed to transform your understanding and practical abilities in working with LangGraph and building autonomous multi-agent systems. Here's a breakdown of the key learning outcomes you can expect from each section:

Part I: Introduction

- **Foundational Knowledge:**
  Learn the history and evolution of autonomous systems, the role of LangGraph, and why graph theory is central to modeling agent interactions.
- **Context and Motivation:**
  Understand the driving forces behind the development of multi-agent systems and see how these systems are applied across various industries.

Part II: Core Concepts and Fundamentals

- **Theoretical Foundations:**
  Gain a solid grasp of core concepts such as autonomous agents, communication protocols, and graph theory basics.
- **Architectural Insights:**
  Delve into the internal workings of LangGraph, exploring its modular design, extensibility, and security features.

Part III: Building Autonomous Systems

- **Design and Implementation:**
  Develop hands-on skills for designing and building multi-agent systems. Step-by-step tutorials and code examples will guide you through creating your own agents and integrating them into a coherent system.
- **Practical Techniques:**
  Learn best practices for coding, testing, and debugging your systems.

Real-world examples will illustrate how to handle complex interactions between agents.

Part IV: Scaling and Optimization

- **Performance Strategies:**
  Discover techniques for scaling your system to handle increased load and ensure high availability. Learn how to profile, benchmark, and optimize system performance.
- **Deployment Best Practices:**
  Understand how to deploy your systems in cloud and distributed environments. This part covers containerization, orchestration, and continuous integration/deployment (CI/CD) pipelines.

Part V: Real-World Applications and Future Directions

- **Industry-Specific Applications:**
  Explore case studies and applications of autonomous systems in robotics, finance, IoT, healthcare, and transportation. See how theory is translated into practice.
- **Future Trends:**
  Stay informed about emerging technologies, ethical considerations, and regulatory challenges. Learn how to future-proof your systems and prepare for upcoming innovations.

Part VI: Appendices and Reference Materials

- **Quick References and Resources:**
  Use the appendices as a go-to resource for installation guides, API references, and a glossary of terms. These materials will support your learning and help you quickly reference key concepts.
- **Extended Learning:**
  Find further reading materials and links to online communities, enabling you to continue your education beyond the scope of this book.

The structure of this book is carefully designed to guide you through the entire lifecycle of working with LangGraph—from understanding the foundational concepts and setting up your environment to building, scaling, and optimizing robust multi-agent systems. As you progress through each part, you will build a comprehensive understanding and gain practical skills that empower you to innovate and excel in real-world applications.

By the end of this journey, you will not only be well-versed in the theory behind autonomous multi-agent systems but will also have the hands-on experience necessary to design, implement, and deploy these systems in various industries. Welcome to your transformative learning experience with LangGraph!

Chapter 2: Getting Started with LangGraph

In this chapter, we will walk through the initial steps required to start working with LangGraph. Whether you are setting up your environment for the first time or looking to create your very first LangGraph application, this chapter provides a detailed, step-by-step guide. We will cover everything from system requirements and installation to configuring your development environment and writing a basic "Hello World" application.

2.1 Installation and Environment Setup

Before diving into coding, it is essential to ensure that your system meets the necessary requirements and that your development environment is properly configured. This section outlines the prerequisites, guides you through the installation process, and shows you how to set up your environment to start working with LangGraph.

System Requirements

To run LangGraph effectively, your computer should meet the following minimum requirements:

Component	Minimum Requirement	Recommended
Operating System	Windows 10, macOS 10.13+, or Linux (any modern distro)	Latest version of your preferred OS
Processor	Dual-core CPU	Quad-core or higher
Memory (RAM)	4 GB	8 GB or more
Disk Space	At least 500 MB available	1 GB or more for development tools and libraries
Python Version	Python 3.8	Python 3.9 or later

Component	Minimum Requirement	Recommended
Internet Connection	Required for downloading packages	Stable high-speed connection for smoother installations

Step-by-Step Installation Guide

Follow these steps to install LangGraph on your system:

1. **Install Python:**
   - **Windows/Mac/Linux:**
     Download and install the latest version of Python (3.8 or higher) from the official Python website.
   - **Verify Installation:**
     Open a terminal (or Command Prompt on Windows) and run:

     bash

     python --version

     Ensure the output shows the correct Python version.

2. **Set Up a Virtual Environment (Recommended):**
   - Creating a virtual environment is a best practice as it isolates your project's dependencies from the system-wide packages.
   - Open your terminal and navigate to your project directory.
   - Create a virtual environment by running:

     bash

     python -m venv env

   - Activate the virtual environment:
     - **Windows:**

       bash

       .\env\Scripts\activate

     - **macOS/Linux:**

```bash
bash
```

```bash
source env/bin/activate
```

- o Once activated, your terminal prompt should show the environment name (e.g., (env)).
3. **Install LangGraph:**
   - o With your virtual environment activated, install LangGraph using pip:

```bash
bash
```

```bash
pip install langgraph
```

   - o This command downloads and installs LangGraph along with any required dependencies.
4. **Verify the Installation:**
   - o To ensure LangGraph is installed correctly, run the following Python command:

```python
python
```

```python
python -c "import langgraph; print('LangGraph installed successfully!')"
```

   - o You should see the message confirming the installation.

Configuring Your Development Environment

After installing LangGraph, configure your development environment to streamline your workflow:

1. **Integrated Development Environment (IDE):**
   - o **Recommendations:**
     - ▪ Visual Studio Code
     - ▪ PyCharm
   - o Configure your IDE to use the virtual environment you created. For example, in VS Code:
     - ▪ Open the Command Palette (Ctrl+Shift+P or Cmd+Shift+P on macOS).
     - ▪ Type Python: Select Interpreter and choose the interpreter located in your env folder.

2. **Code Formatting and Linting:**
   - Set up tools like flake8 or pylint to maintain code quality. Install them using pip:

   bash

   pip install flake8 pylint

   - Configure your IDE to run these tools automatically when you save your files.

3. **Version Control:**
   - Use Git to manage your code. Initialize a repository in your project directory:

   bash

   git init

   - Create a .gitignore file to exclude the virtual environment and other unnecessary files:

   bash

   env/
   __pycache__/
   *.pyc

4. **Documentation and Testing:**
   - Familiarize yourself with LangGraph's documentation available online.
   - Set up a testing framework such as pytest to write and run tests:

   bash

   pip install pytest

   - Create a simple test file to verify that your environment is working as expected.

2.2 Your First LangGraph Application: A "Hello World" Example

Now that your environment is set up, let's create your first LangGraph application—a simple "Hello World" example. This project is designed to introduce you to the basic concepts and workflow of LangGraph.

Overview of the Introductory Project

In this introductory project, you will:

- Create a minimal LangGraph application.
- Define a basic autonomous agent that performs a simple action.
- Learn how to integrate this agent into the LangGraph system.
- Run and test the application to see the output.

This example serves as a foundation upon which you can build more complex systems as you progress through the book.

Code Walkthrough and Explanation

Below is the complete code for the "Hello World" application. We will walk through each part of the code to explain what it does.

python

```python
# hello_world.py

# Import the necessary components from the LangGraph framework
from langgraph import GraphSystem, Agent

# Define a simple autonomous agent class
class HelloWorldAgent(Agent):
    def __init__(self, name):
        # Call the parent constructor to initialize the agent's name
        super().__init__(name)

    def act(self):
        """
        This method is invoked to perform the agent's action.
        In this example, the agent simply prints a greeting message.
        """
        print(f"Hello, World! I am {self.name} and I'm an autonomous agent.")
```

```
# Entry point of the application
if __name__ == "__main__":
    # Create an instance of the LangGraph system
    system = GraphSystem()

    # Instantiate the HelloWorldAgent with a given name
    hello_agent = HelloWorldAgent("HelloAgent")

    # Add the agent to the system
    system.add_agent(hello_agent)

    # Trigger the agent's action
    hello_agent.act()
```

Explanation of the Code:

1. **Imports:**
   - o The code begins by importing the GraphSystem and Agent classes from the LangGraph framework.
   - o These components provide the foundational structure for creating and managing agents.
2. **Defining the Agent:**
   - o The HelloWorldAgent class inherits from the Agent class.
   - o The __init__ method initializes the agent by calling the parent constructor, ensuring the agent is correctly registered with a name.
   - o The act method is defined to perform the agent's primary function—in this case, printing a greeting message to the console.
3. **Setting Up the System:**
   - o In the __main__ block, an instance of GraphSystem is created. This system acts as the environment where agents are managed.
   - o An instance of HelloWorldAgent is then created and added to the system using the add_agent method.
4. **Running the Agent's Action:**
   - o Finally, the act method of the HelloWorldAgent is called, which outputs a "Hello, World!" message along with the agent's name.

Running and Testing Your Application

Once you have written the code, follow these steps to run and test your application:

1. **Save the File:**
   o Save the code above in a file named hello_world.py within your project directory.
2. **Activate Your Virtual Environment (if not already active):**
   o Open your terminal and navigate to the project directory.
   o Activate the virtual environment:
     ▪ **Windows:** .\env\Scripts\activate
     ▪ **macOS/Linux:** source env/bin/activate
3. **Run the Application:**
   o In the terminal, execute the following command:

   bash

   python hello_world.py

   o You should see the following output:

   mathematica

   Hello, World! I am HelloAgent and I'm an autonomous agent.

4. **Testing:**
   o To ensure your application is working as expected, you can modify the message or add additional agents and observe the behavior.
   o For more extensive testing, consider writing unit tests using a framework like pytest.

In this chapter, you have learned how to set up your environment for working with LangGraph and created your first "Hello World" application. By following the step-by-step instructions for installation and configuration, you have laid a solid foundation for further exploration into building autonomous multi-agent systems. With your development environment ready and a basic application running, you are now well-prepared to dive into more advanced topics and practical applications in the upcoming chapters.

2.3 Exploring the LangGraph Interface and Tools

In this section, we explore the various interfaces and tools that LangGraph offers to streamline the development, monitoring, and management of autonomous multi-agent systems. LangGraph is designed not only to simplify the coding process but also to provide robust support through user-friendly dashboards, visualization tools, and a rich set of APIs and plugins that extend its functionality. This section will guide you through these features in detail.

User Interfaces, Dashboards, and Visualization Tools

One of the key strengths of LangGraph is its ability to provide intuitive visual representations of your multi-agent system. These visual tools are essential for debugging, monitoring, and understanding the complex interactions between agents.

Graphical Dashboards

LangGraph comes with a built-in dashboard that allows you to monitor the state of your system in real time. Here are some of the primary features:

- **System Overview:**
  The dashboard displays an overview of all active agents, their statuses, and key performance metrics. This may include the number of active agents, response times, and the current load on the system.
- **Real-Time Graph Visualization:**
  Agents are represented as nodes, and the interactions or communications between them are depicted as edges. This visualization helps in identifying clusters, bottlenecks, or isolated agents that may require attention.
- **Event Logs:**
  A dedicated section for event logs records all significant system events, such as agent actions, communication exchanges, and error notifications. This log is invaluable for troubleshooting and auditing.
- **Performance Metrics:**
  Integrated charts and graphs show CPU usage, memory consumption, network latency, and other performance indicators. These metrics allow you to track system performance over time and adjust resources accordingly.

Interactive Visualization Tools

In addition to dashboards, LangGraph includes several interactive tools designed to help you better understand and manage your system:

- **Node Inspection:**
  Clickable nodes in the graph allow you to inspect individual agents. You can view details such as the agent's current state, historical actions, and resource usage.
- **Path Tracing:**
  Tools that allow you to trace the path of data or commands through the system. This is particularly useful for debugging communication issues or understanding how a specific instruction propagates through the network.
- **Customizable Views:**
  The visualization tools often come with customizable options, allowing you to filter agents by type, status, or performance thresholds. You can zoom in on specific regions of the graph or highlight critical paths.

Example: Visualizing a LangGraph System

Consider a simple multi-agent system where three agents interact. When you launch the LangGraph dashboard, you might see a visualization similar to the following diagram:

css

```
    [Agent A]
      / \
     /   \
[Agent B]---[Agent C]
```

- **Agent A, B, C** are represented as nodes.
- **Edges** represent the communication links between the agents.
- Hovering over a node provides a summary of the agent's status and recent actions.

This visual representation enables you to quickly assess the overall health of your system and pinpoint areas that may need further investigation.

Overview of Available APIs and Plugins

LangGraph's extensibility is one of its most powerful features. It provides a comprehensive set of APIs and supports a wide range of plugins that enhance the capabilities of your multi-agent systems.

Core APIs

The LangGraph framework exposes several APIs that allow you to interact with the system programmatically. These APIs facilitate tasks such as creating agents, sending messages, and querying system status. Below is an overview of some core API functionalities:

API Functionality	Description	Example Usage
Agent Creation	Instantiate and configure new agents within the system.	agent = Agent("Agent Name")
Message Passing	Send and receive messages between agents.	agent.send("Hello", target=other_agent)
System Query	Retrieve the current status of agents and the overall system health.	system.get_status()
Event Subscription	Subscribe to specific events (e.g., error, communication complete).	system.subscribe("error", error_handler_function)
Performance Metrics	Access real-time performance data and logs.	metrics = system.get_performance_metrics()

Plugin Architecture

LangGraph supports a plugin architecture that allows developers to extend its functionality without modifying the core framework. Plugins can add new features such as advanced analytics, additional communication protocols, or integrations with external services. Here are some common plugin categories:

- **Visualization Plugins:**
  Enhance the dashboard with custom charts or third-party visualization libraries. For example, a plugin might integrate with D3.js to provide interactive graphs.
- **Communication Plugins:**
  Extend support for additional protocols (e.g., MQTT, WebSockets) to enable more diverse communication strategies between agents.
- **Analytics and Monitoring Plugins:**
  Provide advanced data analysis, anomaly detection, and automated alerts. These plugins can integrate with tools like Prometheus or Grafana for detailed performance monitoring.
- **Integration Plugins:**
  Connect LangGraph to external systems such as databases, cloud services, or IoT platforms. This enables seamless data exchange and system interoperability.

Example: Using a Plugin to Enhance Visualization

Imagine you want to integrate a plugin that uses the Plotly library for enhanced interactive charts. The following example demonstrates how you might configure such a plugin:

1. **Install the Plugin:**

bash

pip install langgraph-plotly-plugin

2. **Configure the Plugin in Your Application:**

python

```
# Import the plugin
from langgraph.plugins.plotly_visualizer import PlotlyVisualizer

# Create an instance of the Plotly visualizer
visualizer = PlotlyVisualizer()

# Integrate the visualizer with your LangGraph system
system.register_visualizer(visualizer)
```

Now, when you run the system, the enhanced visualization dashboard will be available.

Explanation:

- The code first installs the plugin via pip.
- It then imports the PlotlyVisualizer from the plugin package.
- An instance of the visualizer is created and registered with the LangGraph system, enabling enhanced visualization features on your dashboard.

In this section, we explored the powerful interfaces and tools that LangGraph provides to help you manage and monitor your multi-agent systems. The user interfaces, dashboards, and visualization tools offer intuitive and interactive ways to understand system behavior, while the comprehensive APIs and flexible plugin architecture allow you to extend and customize LangGraph to fit your specific needs.

With these tools at your disposal, you can more easily design, debug, and optimize complex systems. As you continue to work with LangGraph, these features will become indispensable in ensuring that your autonomous multi-agent systems are efficient, scalable, and robust.

Chapter 3: Fundamentals of Autonomous Multi-Agent Systems

In this chapter, we lay the groundwork for understanding autonomous multi-agent systems. We will begin by defining what autonomous agents are, exploring their inherent characteristics and capabilities. Then, we will dive into the various behaviors these agents exhibit and how they interact with one another through distinct models and decision-making processes. This foundational knowledge is critical for building, managing, and scaling complex systems where multiple agents operate in concert.

3.1 Defining Autonomous Agents

Autonomous agents are the fundamental building blocks of multi-agent systems. They are self-directed entities capable of making decisions, interacting with their environment, and collaborating with other agents to achieve specific goals. Understanding their characteristics and capabilities is essential for designing systems that are both efficient and adaptable.

Characteristics of Autonomous Agents

Autonomous agents exhibit several key characteristics:

- **Autonomy:**
  Agents operate independently without direct human intervention. They can initiate actions based on their own perceptions and internal goals.
- **Reactivity:**
  Agents are designed to respond to changes in their environment. They continuously monitor their surroundings and react accordingly to new events or stimuli.
- **Proactiveness:**
  Beyond mere reaction, agents can take initiative by planning and executing actions that further their objectives, rather than only responding to environmental changes.
- **Social Ability:**
  Autonomous agents can communicate and collaborate with other

agents. They exchange information, negotiate, and coordinate actions to achieve complex tasks.

- **Adaptability:**
Agents are often designed to learn from their experiences. They adjust their behaviors based on feedback, evolving over time to improve performance.

Capabilities of Autonomous Agents

The capabilities of autonomous agents can be broadly categorized as follows:

- **Perception:**
Agents gather data from their environment using sensors or data inputs. This information is processed to form an internal representation of the external world.
- **Decision Making:**
Based on their perceptions, agents decide on a course of action. Decision-making can be rule-based, probabilistic, or driven by machine learning techniques.
- **Action Execution:**
Once a decision is made, agents perform actions that affect the environment or communicate with other agents. This might include moving, manipulating objects, or transmitting messages.
- **Communication:**
Communication is essential for multi-agent coordination. Agents use established protocols or custom APIs to share information, request assistance, or synchronize their activities.

Summary Table of Characteristics and Capabilities

Characteristic/Capability	Description	Example in Multi-Agent Systems
Autonomy	Operates independently based on internal goals and perceptions.	A drone navigating an environment without human control.
Reactivity	Responds to changes in the environment in real time.	A sensor-equipped robot stopping when an obstacle is detected.

Characteristic/Capability	Description	Example in Multi-Agent Systems
Proactiveness	Initiates actions based on planning and goal setting.	An automated system scheduling maintenance tasks before failures occur.
Social Ability	Communicates and collaborates with other agents.	Agents in a network sharing real-time data for coordinated responses.
Adaptability	Adjusts behavior based on feedback and learning.	A trading agent updating its strategy after market fluctuations.
Perception	Gathers environmental data using sensors or data inputs.	A security system using cameras and motion sensors to monitor premises.
Decision Making	Processes information and decides on a course of action.	A home automation agent determining optimal energy usage.
Action Execution	Performs physical or digital actions to influence the environment.	An industrial robot assembling components on a production line.
Communication	Exchanges information with other agents and systems.	Autonomous vehicles sharing road condition data.

3.2 Agent Behaviors and Interaction Models

Autonomous agents are not static; they exhibit a range of behaviors that define how they act and interact within a system. In this section, we explore the behavioral patterns and decision-making processes that govern these agents, as well as the interaction models that facilitate communication and coordination among them.

Behavioral Patterns

Agents can exhibit various types of behaviors based on their design and the tasks they are meant to perform. The most common behavioral patterns include:

- **Reactive Behavior:**
  Agents respond immediately to environmental stimuli. These agents do not engage in long-term planning but are efficient in dynamic environments where rapid response is critical.
  Example: A robotic vacuum that changes direction upon encountering an obstacle.
- **Deliberative Behavior:**
  These agents plan their actions by considering future consequences and multiple potential outcomes. They weigh different options before deciding on an action.
  Example: An autonomous vehicle planning its route by considering traffic conditions and road hazards.
- **Hybrid Behavior:**
  A combination of reactive and deliberative behaviors, where an agent reacts to immediate changes while also planning for future events.
  Example: A drone that reacts to sudden weather changes while following a predefined flight plan.

Decision-Making Processes

The decision-making process of an agent determines how it chooses a course of action from available options. Common decision-making models include:

- **Rule-Based Systems:**
  Agents follow a set of predefined rules or conditions.
  Example Code Snippet:

```python
def decide_action(environment_data):
    # Simple rule-based decision: if temperature is high, turn on cooling system.
    if environment_data['temperature'] > 30:
        return "activate_cooling"
    else:
        return "maintain_state"
```

```
# Example environment data
environment_data = {'temperature': 32}
action = decide_action(environment_data)
print(f"Decided Action: {action}")
```

Explanation:
This snippet defines a simple rule-based decision function where the agent activates a cooling system if the temperature exceeds 30°C.

- **Utility-Based Decision Making:**
  Agents assign a utility value to each possible action based on expected outcomes and select the action with the highest utility.
  Example: An agent choosing between different paths where each path is scored based on distance, safety, and energy consumption.
- **Belief-Desire-Intention (BDI) Model:**
  A cognitive approach where agents operate based on their beliefs (information about the world), desires (objectives or goals), and intentions (committed plans to achieve those goals).
  Example: An agent in a logistics network that believes a delivery truck is delayed, desires to minimize waiting time, and intends to reroute resources accordingly.
- **Learning-Based Approaches:**
  Agents utilize machine learning techniques, such as reinforcement learning, to improve their decision-making over time by learning from past experiences.
  Example: An agent optimizing energy consumption by learning the most efficient operating patterns in a smart grid.

Interaction Models

The interaction among agents is crucial for the success of multi-agent systems. Several models exist to facilitate communication and collaboration:

- **Message Passing:**
  Agents communicate by sending discrete messages to one another. This is a common and straightforward interaction model.
  Example Code Snippet:

```python
class Agent:
```

```python
    def __init__(self, name):
        self.name = name

    def send_message(self, message, recipient):
        print(f"{self.name} sends message to {recipient.name}: {message}")

    def receive_message(self, message, sender):
        print(f"{self.name} received message from {sender.name}: {message}")

# Create two agents and simulate a message passing scenario
agent_A = Agent("Agent A")
agent_B = Agent("Agent B")
agent_A.send_message("Hello, Agent B!", agent_B)
agent_B.receive_message("Hello, Agent B!", agent_A)
```

Explanation:
This code demonstrates a simple message-passing mechanism where one agent sends a message to another, which then receives and prints the message.

- **Event-Driven Communication:**
  Agents trigger events that other agents subscribe to. This model is useful for asynchronous communication where agents do not need to be directly connected.
- **Shared Memory or Blackboard Systems:**
  Multiple agents access and modify a common data repository. This model allows for a centralized approach to sharing information.
- **Broker-Based Models:**
  A mediator (or broker) facilitates communication between agents, managing message routing and ensuring that data is delivered efficiently.

Summary Table of Interaction Models

Interaction Model	Description	Advantages	Example Use Case
Message Passing	Direct communication via	Simple and direct; easy to implement.	Chat applications among robots.

Interaction Model	Description	Advantages	Example Use Case
	discrete messages between agents.		
Event-Driven	Communication via event notifications to which agents subscribe.	Asynchronous; decouples sender and receiver.	Real-time alert systems.
Shared Memory	Agents share a common repository for data.	Centralized data access; easy to maintain consistency.	Collaborative problem-solving tasks.
Broker-Based	A central broker manages and routes communication between agents.	Scalable; decouples agents from communication logic.	Distributed systems like financial transaction networks.

In this chapter, we have defined what autonomous agents are by examining their key characteristics and capabilities. We have also explored the diverse behavioral patterns and decision-making processes that drive agent actions within a multi-agent system. Furthermore, we examined various interaction models that enable effective communication and collaboration among agents.

Understanding these fundamentals is essential for designing systems that are both robust and scalable. As you move forward, these concepts will form the basis upon which you will build more complex and capable autonomous multi-agent systems using LangGraph.

3.3 Communication Protocols in Multi-Agent Systems

Effective communication is the lifeblood of multi-agent systems. In distributed environments, agents must exchange data, coordinate actions, and make joint decisions. In this section, we discuss the primary communication protocols used in such systems, focusing on message passing, event-driven communication, and distributed decision making with consensus algorithms.

Message Passing and Event-Driven Communication

Message Passing

Message passing is a fundamental communication method where agents exchange discrete messages. Each message typically contains instructions, data, or status updates. This approach is favored for its simplicity and directness.

Key Features:

- **Direct Communication:** Agents send messages directly to other agents.
- **Synchronous or Asynchronous:** Communication can be blocking (waiting for a response) or non-blocking.
- **Encapsulation:** Each message encapsulates data, ensuring that the sender and receiver interact through well-defined interfaces.

Example: Simple Message Passing in Python

Below is a code snippet demonstrating basic message passing between two agents.

python

```python
class Agent:
    def __init__(self, name):
        self.name = name

    def send_message(self, message, recipient):
        """Send a message to another agent."""
        print(f"{self.name} sends to {recipient.name}: {message}")
        recipient.receive_message(message, self)

    def receive_message(self, message, sender):
        """Receive a message from another agent."""
        print(f"{self.name} received from {sender.name}: {message}")

# Create two agents
agent_A = Agent("Agent A")
agent_B = Agent("Agent B")
```

```python
# Agent A sends a message to Agent B
agent_A.send_message("Hello from Agent A!", agent_B)
```

Explanation:

- The Agent class includes methods for sending and receiving messages.
- When agent_A sends a message to agent_B, the message is printed to the console from both the sender's and receiver's perspectives.

Event-Driven Communication

Event-driven communication shifts the focus from direct message exchanges to events that agents emit. Other agents subscribe to these events and act when an event occurs.

Key Features:

- **Asynchronous:** Agents do not need to be actively waiting for messages; they simply react when an event occurs.
- **Decoupling:** Producers (emitters) and consumers (subscribers) are decoupled, leading to flexible system design.
- **Scalability:** Event-driven architectures can handle a high volume of events and support many agents concurrently.

Example: Basic Event-Driven Communication in Python

Below is a simple implementation of an event-driven system using a central event dispatcher.

python

```python
class EventDispatcher:
    def __init__(self):
        self.subscribers = {}

    def subscribe(self, event_type, handler):
        """Subscribe a handler to a specific event type."""
        if event_type not in self.subscribers:
            self.subscribers[event_type] = []
        self.subscribers[event_type].append(handler)
```

```python
    def publish(self, event_type, data):
        """Publish an event to all subscribers."""
        if event_type in self.subscribers:
            for handler in self.subscribers[event_type]:
                handler(data)

# Define two example handlers
def handle_temperature_change(data):
    print(f"Temperature handler: The temperature is now {data}°C.")

def handle_humidity_change(data):
    print(f"Humidity handler: The humidity is now {data}%.")

# Create an event dispatcher
dispatcher = EventDispatcher()

# Subscribe handlers to events
dispatcher.subscribe("temperature_change", handle_temperature_change)
dispatcher.subscribe("humidity_change", handle_humidity_change)

# Publish events
dispatcher.publish("temperature_change", 25)
dispatcher.publish("humidity_change", 60)
```

Explanation:

- The EventDispatcher class manages subscriptions and publishes events to registered handlers.
- Handlers (handle_temperature_change and handle_humidity_change) are functions that process event data.
- When events are published, all subscribers to that event type receive the notification and act accordingly.

Distributed Decision Making and Consensus Algorithms

In multi-agent systems, individual agents often need to collaborate and agree on decisions that affect the entire system. Distributed decision making involves methods and protocols that ensure agents arrive at a consensus, even when operating in a decentralized environment.

Distributed Decision Making

This process involves each agent contributing its local information and preferences, which are then aggregated to make a collective decision. Techniques include:

- **Voting Systems:** Agents vote on preferred actions, and the majority decision is implemented.
- **Utility Aggregation:** Each agent assigns a utility value to possible outcomes, and the option with the highest total utility is selected.

Consensus Algorithms

Consensus algorithms ensure that all agents in a distributed system agree on a single data value or course of action. These algorithms are critical in environments where reliability and consistency are paramount.

Common Consensus Algorithms:

- **Paxos:**
  A family of protocols designed to achieve consensus in a network of unreliable processors.
- **Raft:**
  An alternative to Paxos that is easier to understand and implement, often used in distributed databases.
- **Byzantine Fault Tolerance (BFT):**
  Algorithms that ensure consensus even in the presence of malicious agents or failures, e.g., Practical Byzantine Fault Tolerance (PBFT).

Example: Simulating a Simple Consensus Process

Below is a simplified example using a voting mechanism where agents agree on a decision based on a majority vote.

python

```
def majority_vote(votes):
    """
    Determine the decision based on a simple majority vote.
    :param votes: List of votes (strings).
    :return: The decision with the most votes.
    """
```

```
vote_count = {}
for vote in votes:
    vote_count[vote] = vote_count.get(vote, 0) + 1
# Determine the decision with the maximum votes
decision = max(vote_count, key=vote_count.get)
return decision

# Example votes from agents
votes = ["Option A", "Option B", "Option A", "Option A", "Option B"]

# Calculate the consensus decision
consensus = majority_vote(votes)
print(f"Consensus Decision: {consensus}")
```

Explanation:

- The function majority_vote aggregates votes from agents.
- In this example, agents vote for "Option A" or "Option B".
- The option with the majority of votes is selected as the consensus decision.

Comparison Table of Communication Protocols and Consensus Approaches

Aspect	Message Passing	Event-Driven Communication	Consensus Algorithms
Mode of Operation	Direct, synchronous or asynchronous messages	Asynchronous event publication and subscription	Iterative decision making through voting or utility aggregation
Decoupling	Low decoupling (direct agent-to-agent communication)	High decoupling between event producers and consumers	Decoupling depends on the algorithm, but aims for global agreement
Scalability	Moderate, may require additional handling for high volumes	High, naturally supports many agents and events	Varies; algorithms like Raft are designed for scalable environments

Aspect	Message Passing	Event-Driven Communication	Consensus Algorithms
Fault Tolerance	Basic error handling via message retries	Improved through event buffering and handling	High, designed to achieve consensus despite failures or malicious behavior
Use Cases	Simple command and control scenarios	Real-time monitoring, alert systems	Distributed databases, blockchain networks, coordinated decision making

3.4 Scalability and Resilience in Autonomous Systems

As multi-agent systems grow, they must be able to handle increased loads and recover from failures without compromising performance. Scalability and resilience are key attributes that ensure systems remain efficient and robust, even in the face of unexpected challenges.

Handling Growth in Distributed Environments

Scalability Techniques

Scalability refers to a system's ability to handle an increasing number of agents and interactions. Several techniques can be employed:

- **Horizontal Scaling:**
  Adding more nodes or agents to distribute the workload. This can be done by partitioning tasks among agents or deploying additional instances of the system.
- **Load Balancing:**
  Distributing incoming requests evenly across multiple agents or servers. Load balancing can be achieved using dedicated hardware or software solutions (e.g., HAProxy, NGINX).
- **Modular Architecture:**
  Designing systems in a modular way where components (or modules) can be independently scaled. For example, separating the processing layer from the communication layer allows for targeted scaling.

- **Caching Mechanisms:**
  Utilizing caching strategies to reduce redundant computations and data retrieval. This is especially useful in systems with frequent read operations.

Example: Horizontal Scaling Concept

Consider a distributed system where agents are responsible for processing incoming data streams. As the volume of data increases, you can horizontally scale by deploying additional agent instances to share the load.

python

```python
class ProcessingAgent(Agent):
    def process_data(self, data):
        # Simulate data processing
        print(f"{self.name} processing data: {data}")

# Simulate deploying multiple processing agents
agents = [ProcessingAgent(f"Agent {i}") for i in range(1, 4)]

# Distribute incoming data among agents in a round-robin fashion
data_stream = ["Data1", "Data2", "Data3", "Data4", "Data5"]
for index, data in enumerate(data_stream):
    agent = agents[index % len(agents)]
    agent.process_data(data)
```

Explanation:

- Three processing agents are created.
- Data is distributed among the agents in a round-robin manner, ensuring that the workload is balanced as more data arrives.

Resilience in Autonomous Systems

Resilience is the ability of a system to maintain functionality and recover quickly from failures. In distributed multi-agent systems, resilience is achieved through:

- **Redundancy:**
  Having multiple agents or nodes performing the same function so that if one fails, others can take over.

- **Failover Mechanisms:**
  Automated processes that detect failures and switch operations to standby agents or backup systems.
- **Self-Healing Architectures:**
  Systems that monitor their own performance and can automatically recover from issues by restarting components or reallocating resources.
- **Distributed Data Replication:**
  Ensuring that critical data is replicated across multiple nodes to prevent data loss during failures.

Strategies to Handle Failures

Example: Simple Failover Simulation

python

```python
class ResilientAgent(Agent):
    def __init__(self, name):
        super().__init__(name)
        self.active = True

    def perform_task(self):
        if self.active:
            print(f"{self.name} is performing its task.")
        else:
            print(f"{self.name} is offline. Task cannot be performed.")

    def fail(self):
        self.active = False
        print(f"{self.name} has failed!")

    def recover(self):
        self.active = True
        print(f"{self.name} has recovered and is back online.")

# Create an agent and simulate failure and recovery
resilient_agent = ResilientAgent("ResilientAgent 1")
resilient_agent.perform_task()
resilient_agent.fail()
resilient_agent.perform_task()
resilient_agent.recover()
```

resilient_agent.perform_task()

Explanation:

- The ResilientAgent class extends the basic Agent with methods to simulate failure and recovery.
- The agent's ability to perform tasks is dependent on its active status.
- The simulation shows the agent performing a task, failing, being unable to perform the task, and finally recovering.

Summary Table: Scalability and Resilience Techniques

Aspect	Technique	Benefits	Example Use Case
Scalability	Horizontal Scaling	Distributes workload among more agents	Handling increased web traffic or data streams.
	Load Balancing	Ensures even distribution of requests	Web server clusters in cloud environments.
	Modular Architecture	Facilitates independent scaling of system components	Microservices architecture.
	Caching	Reduces redundant processing and speeds up data retrieval	Content delivery networks (CDNs).
Resilience	Redundancy	Provides backup agents to take over in case of failure	Fault-tolerant database clusters.
	Failover Mechanisms	Automatically switches to standby systems upon failures	High-availability systems in financial services.
	Self-Healing Architectures	Monitors system health and automatically recovers from faults	Cloud orchestration platforms.
	Distributed Data Replication	Prevents data loss by storing copies on multiple nodes	Distributed file systems.

In this section, we have explored the crucial communication protocols that underpin effective multi-agent systems. We discussed both message passing and event-driven communication, demonstrating how agents can interact directly or through an event-based architecture. We also reviewed distributed decision-making techniques and consensus algorithms that allow agents to arrive at shared decisions in a decentralized environment.

Following this, we examined the strategies for ensuring scalability and resilience in autonomous systems. By implementing techniques such as horizontal scaling, load balancing, redundancy, and failover mechanisms, systems can handle increased loads and recover gracefully from failures.

Together, these protocols and strategies form the backbone of robust, efficient, and scalable multi-agent systems, providing the necessary framework for developing advanced applications using LangGraph. Armed with these concepts, you are now better equipped to design and implement systems that can meet the demands of modern, distributed environments.

Chapter 4: Graph Theory Essentials for LangGraph

Graph theory is a fundamental field of mathematics that provides powerful tools to model, analyze, and visualize complex relationships. In the context of LangGraph, graph theory is used to represent autonomous agents and their interactions. This chapter introduces the basic concepts of graph theory and explains how to map system components into graph elements.

4.1 Basic Concepts in Graph Theory

In this section, we will cover the foundational elements of graph theory, including nodes, edges, and various graph types.

Nodes (Vertices)

- **Definition:**
  A **node** (or vertex) is the fundamental unit in a graph. It represents an individual entity or object. In multi-agent systems, each node typically corresponds to an autonomous agent.
- **Attributes:**
  Nodes can store various attributes such as a unique identifier, status, position, or any other metadata relevant to the system. These attributes help in distinguishing one agent from another and in managing their behaviors.

Edges

- **Definition:**
  An **edge** is a connection between two nodes that represents a relationship or interaction. In the context of autonomous systems, an edge might represent communication, collaboration, or dependency between agents.
- **Types of Edges:**
  - **Undirected Edges:**
    Indicate a bidirectional relationship. For example, in a friendship network, the connection between two friends is mutual.

- o **Directed Edges (Arcs):**
  Indicate a one-way relationship. For example, in a Twitter-like follow network, if Agent A follows Agent B, the edge points from Agent A to Agent B.
- **Weighted Edges:**
  Sometimes, edges carry a numerical value (or weight) that quantifies the strength, cost, or capacity of the relationship. For instance, in a road network, the weight might represent the distance between intersections.

Graph Types

1. **Undirected Graph:**
   A graph where all edges are undirected, meaning the connection between any two nodes is bidirectional.

   Example:
   A network of collaborating agents where every relationship is mutual.

2. **Directed Graph (Digraph):**
   A graph where edges have a specific direction, indicating the flow of information or control from one node to another.

   Example:
   A command-and-control system where instructions flow from a central command agent to subordinate agents.

3. **Weighted Graph:**
   A graph in which edges have associated weights.

   Example:
   A network of sensors where the weight represents the latency or reliability of the communication channel between sensors.

Example Code: Creating Basic Graphs with NetworkX

Below is an example in Python using the NetworkX library to create and visualize both an undirected and a directed graph.

python

```
import networkx as nx
```

```python
import matplotlib.pyplot as plt

# Create an undirected graph
G_undirected = nx.Graph()

# Add nodes representing agents
G_undirected.add_node("Agent A")
G_undirected.add_node("Agent B")
G_undirected.add_node("Agent C")

# Add edges representing mutual relationships
G_undirected.add_edge("Agent A", "Agent B")
G_undirected.add_edge("Agent A", "Agent C")
G_undirected.add_edge("Agent B", "Agent C")

# Visualize the undirected graph
plt.figure(figsize=(6, 4))
nx.draw(G_undirected, with_labels=True, node_color='lightblue',
edge_color='gray', node_size=1500, font_size=12)
plt.title("Undirected Graph Example")
plt.show()

# Create a directed graph
G_directed = nx.DiGraph()

# Add nodes
G_directed.add_node("Agent A")
G_directed.add_node("Agent B")
G_directed.add_node("Agent C")

# Add directed edges
G_directed.add_edge("Agent A", "Agent B")
G_directed.add_edge("Agent B", "Agent C")
G_directed.add_edge("Agent C", "Agent A")

# Visualize the directed graph
plt.figure(figsize=(6, 4))
nx.draw(G_directed, with_labels=True, node_color='lightgreen',
edge_color='black', node_size=1500, font_size=12, arrows=True)
plt.title("Directed Graph Example")
plt.show()
```

Explanation:

- **Undirected Graph:**
    - A graph is created using nx.Graph().
    - Nodes ("Agent A", "Agent B", and "Agent C") are added.
    - Edges are added to indicate mutual connections between the agents.
    - The graph is visualized with a title, clear labels, and a simple layout.
- **Directed Graph:**
    - A graph is created using nx.DiGraph().
    - Nodes are added similarly, and directed edges are introduced to show one-way relationships.
    - The visualization uses arrows to denote the direction of each connection.

Summary Table of Basic Graph Elements

Element	Description	Example
Node (Vertex)	Represents an entity or agent in a system.	"Agent A", "Agent B"
Edge	Represents a connection between two nodes.	An edge connecting "Agent A" and "Agent B".
Undirected Graph	A graph with bidirectional relationships.	A network of mutual collaborators.
Directed Graph	A graph with unidirectional relationships, represented by arrows.	A system where commands flow from one agent to another.
Weighted Graph	A graph where each edge has a numerical value indicating cost or strength.	A road network with distances as weights.

4.2 Representing Agents and Relationships as Graphs

In multi-agent systems, the complex interactions between various autonomous agents can be effectively modeled using graph structures. In this section, we describe how to map the components of a multi-agent system to the elements of a graph.

Mapping Agents to Nodes

- **Representation:**
  Each autonomous agent in your system is represented by a node. This node can include attributes such as:
    - **Name or ID:** Uniquely identifies the agent.
    - **Status:** Indicates whether the agent is active, idle, or offline.
    - **Additional Attributes:** Could include location, capabilities, or performance metrics.
- **Benefits:**
  Representing agents as nodes simplifies the visualization and management of complex systems. It provides a clear, modular view of individual entities within the system.

Mapping Relationships to Edges

- **Representation:**
  Relationships or interactions between agents are represented as edges. An edge can denote various types of interactions, such as:
    - **Communication:** An edge indicates that two agents can exchange messages.
    - **Collaboration:** An edge might show that two agents work together on a task.
    - **Dependency:** An edge can indicate that one agent's operation depends on another's.
- **Attributes of Edges:**
  Edges can carry additional information, such as:
    - **Type of Relationship:** (e.g., "communicates", "collaborates")
    - **Weight:** Indicates the strength or capacity of the interaction (e.g., frequency of communication, reliability of connection).

Example: Representing a Multi-Agent System as a Graph

Below is an example that demonstrates how to represent a multi-agent system using graph elements. We will create a graph where nodes represent agents with specific attributes and edges represent different types of interactions.

python

```python
# Create a graph to represent a multi-agent system
multi_agent_graph = nx.Graph()

# Add nodes representing agents with attributes
multi_agent_graph.add_node("Agent 1", status="active", location="Sector A")
multi_agent_graph.add_node("Agent 2", status="idle", location="Sector B")
multi_agent_graph.add_node("Agent 3", status="active", location="Sector C")
multi_agent_graph.add_node("Agent 4", status="active", location="Sector A")

# Add edges representing relationships between agents
multi_agent_graph.add_edge("Agent 1", "Agent 2", relationship="communicates")
multi_agent_graph.add_edge("Agent 1", "Agent 3", relationship="collaborates")
multi_agent_graph.add_edge("Agent 2", "Agent 4", relationship="communicates")
multi_agent_graph.add_edge("Agent 3", "Agent 4", relationship="collaborates")

# Visualize the multi-agent system graph
plt.figure(figsize=(8, 6))
pos = nx.spring_layout(multi_agent_graph)  # Use spring layout for a clear visual structure
nx.draw(multi_agent_graph, pos, with_labels=True, node_color='lightcoral', edge_color='blue', node_size=2000, font_size=12)

# Draw edge labels to show the type of relationships
edge_labels = nx.get_edge_attributes(multi_agent_graph, 'relationship')
nx.draw_networkx_edge_labels(multi_agent_graph, pos, edge_labels=edge_labels, font_color='red')

plt.title("Multi-Agent System Represented as a Graph")
plt.show()
```

Explanation:

- **Nodes with Attributes:**
  Four agents are added to the graph, each with attributes such as status and location. This enriches the data and aids in analysis.
- **Edges with Relationship Types:**
  Edges are added to represent interactions between the agents. Each edge includes a relationship attribute that specifies the nature of the connection (e.g., "communicates" or "collaborates").
- **Visualization:**
  The spring_layout is used to position the nodes in a visually appealing manner. Edge labels are added to clearly indicate the type of relationship between nodes.

Summary Table: Mapping System Components to Graph Elements

System Component	Graph Element	Attributes/Details
Agent	Node	Unique ID/Name, status (active, idle), location, capabilities
Relationship	Edge	Type (e.g., communicates, collaborates), weight (if applicable)
Overall System	Graph	Represents the entire multi-agent network and its interactions

In this chapter, we explored the essentials of graph theory as they apply to LangGraph. We began by defining the basic elements of graphs—nodes, edges, and various types of graphs (undirected, directed, and weighted)—and provided practical examples using Python's NetworkX library. Next, we discussed how to represent agents and their relationships as graph elements, highlighting the benefits of visualizing multi-agent systems in this structured way.

With these foundational concepts in graph theory, you are now well-equipped to model and analyze the complex interactions within autonomous multi-agent systems. This knowledge serves as a crucial stepping stone as you move forward to more advanced topics in LangGraph.

4.3 Graph Traversal and Search Algorithms

Graph traversal and search algorithms are fundamental tools in graph theory. They allow you to systematically explore the nodes and edges of a graph, which is critical for tasks such as finding a particular node, computing the shortest path, or understanding the structure of a network. In this section, we discuss three common search strategies: Breadth-first search (BFS), Depth-first search (DFS), and heuristic searches (such as A* search).

Breadth-First Search (BFS)

Overview:
Breadth-first search explores a graph level by level starting from a given source node. It visits all neighbors of the source node first, then moves on to the neighbors of those neighbors, and so on. This algorithm is especially useful for finding the shortest path (in terms of the number of edges) in unweighted graphs.

Key Characteristics:

- **Layered Exploration:** Visits nodes in waves based on their distance from the source.
- **Queue Data Structure:** Utilizes a first-in, first-out (FIFO) queue to manage the order of node visits.
- **Completeness:** BFS guarantees finding a solution if one exists (in finite graphs).

Example Code (Python):

python

```
from collections import deque

def bfs(graph, start):
    """
    Perform Breadth-First Search on a graph.

    Parameters:
    - graph: A dictionary representing the graph where keys are nodes and
values are lists of adjacent nodes.
```

- start: The starting node for BFS.

Returns:
- visited: A list of nodes in the order they were visited.
"""
visited = []
queue = deque([start])

while queue:
    current = queue.popleft()
    if current not in visited:
        visited.append(current)
        # Enqueue all adjacent nodes that haven't been visited yet.
        for neighbor in graph.get(current, []):
            if neighbor not in visited:
                queue.append(neighbor)
return visited

```python
# Example graph represented as an adjacency list.
graph_example = {
    'A': ['B', 'C'],
    'B': ['D', 'E'],
    'C': ['F'],
    'D': [],
    'E': ['F'],
    'F': []
}

# Run BFS starting from node 'A'
bfs_result = bfs(graph_example, 'A')
print("BFS Traversal Order:", bfs_result)
```

Explanation:

- The graph is represented as a dictionary where each key is a node, and its value is a list of adjacent nodes.
- A deque is used as a queue to maintain the order of node processing.
- The algorithm continues until all reachable nodes are visited.

Depth-First Search (DFS)

Overview:
Depth-first search explores a graph by moving as deep as possible along each branch before backtracking. This method is often implemented using recursion or a stack. DFS is useful for tasks like detecting cycles, topological sorting, and exploring all possible paths.

Key Characteristics:

- **Deep Exploration:** Follows a single branch to its deepest extent before moving to another branch.
- **Stack Data Structure:** Can be implemented using a stack (or via recursion, which uses the call stack).
- **Memory Efficiency:** DFS typically requires less memory than BFS when dealing with very large graphs (provided the recursion depth is manageable).

Example Code (Python):

python

```python
def dfs(graph, start, visited=None):
    """
    Perform Depth-First Search on a graph.

    Parameters:
    - graph: A dictionary representing the graph.
    - start: The starting node for DFS.
    - visited: A set to keep track of visited nodes.

    Returns:
    - visited_order: A list of nodes in the order they were visited.
    """
    if visited is None:
        visited = set()
    visited.add(start)
    visited_order = [start]

    for neighbor in graph.get(start, []):
        if neighbor not in visited:
            visited_order.extend(dfs(graph, neighbor, visited))
```

```
    return visited_order

# Run DFS starting from node 'A'
dfs_result = dfs(graph_example, 'A')
print("DFS Traversal Order:", dfs_result)
```

Explanation:

- The DFS function uses recursion to traverse as deep as possible from the starting node.
- A set named visited ensures that each node is processed only once.
- The traversal order is maintained in the visited_order list.

Heuristic Searches (A* Search)

Overview:

Heuristic search algorithms use additional information, called heuristics, to guide the search process toward a goal more efficiently. A* search is one of the most popular heuristic algorithms, particularly useful for finding the shortest path in weighted graphs. It combines the actual distance traveled with an estimated distance to the goal.

Key Characteristics:

- **Cost Function:** A* uses a function $f(n)=g(n)+h(n)f(n) = g(n) + h(n)f(n)=g(n)+h(n)$ where:
  - $g(n)g(n)g(n)$ is the cost from the start node to the current node nnn.
  - $h(n)h(n)h(n)$ is the heuristic estimate of the cost from nnn to the goal.
- **Priority Queue:** Uses a priority queue to select the node with the lowest estimated total cost.
- **Optimality:** A* is optimal if the heuristic $h(n)h(n)h(n)$ is admissible (never overestimates the true cost).

Example Code (Python):

python

import heapq

```python
def a_star_search(graph, start, goal, heuristic):
    """
    Perform A* search on a graph to find the shortest path from start to goal.

    Parameters:
    - graph: A dictionary where keys are nodes and values are lists of tuples
    (neighbor, cost).
    - start: The starting node.
    - goal: The target node.
    - heuristic: A function that estimates the cost from a node to the goal.

    Returns:
    - path: A list representing the shortest path from start to goal.
    """
    open_set = []
    heapq.heappush(open_set, (0, start))

    came_from = {}
    g_score = {start: 0}

    while open_set:
        current_f, current = heapq.heappop(open_set)

        if current == goal:
            # Reconstruct the path from start to goal.
            path = []
            while current in came_from:
                path.append(current)
                current = came_from[current]
            path.append(start)
            path.reverse()
            return path

        for neighbor, cost in graph.get(current, []):
            tentative_g_score = g_score[current] + cost
            if tentative_g_score < g_score.get(neighbor, float('inf')):
                came_from[neighbor] = current
                g_score[neighbor] = tentative_g_score
                f_score = tentative_g_score + heuristic(neighbor, goal)
                heapq.heappush(open_set, (f_score, neighbor))
```

```
    return None

# Example weighted graph
weighted_graph = {
    'A': [('B', 1), ('C', 4)],
    'B': [('C', 2), ('D', 5)],
    'C': [('D', 1)],
    'D': []
}

# Heuristic function (for demonstration, using a simple constant heuristic)
def simple_heuristic(node, goal):
    heuristic_values = {'A': 3, 'B': 2, 'C': 1, 'D': 0}
    return heuristic_values.get(node, 0)

# Run A* search from 'A' to 'D'
a_star_path = a_star_search(weighted_graph, 'A', 'D', simple_heuristic)
print("A* Path:", a_star_path)
```

Explanation:

- The A* search function uses a priority queue (implemented with heapq) to manage the open set.
- The came_from dictionary is used to reconstruct the final path once the goal is reached.
- The g_score dictionary stores the cost from the start node to each node.
- The heuristic function provides an estimate of the distance from any node to the goal.
- The example demonstrates finding the shortest path from node 'A' to node 'D' in a weighted graph.

Summary Table: Graph Traversal Algorithms

Algorithm	Data Structure Used	Key Feature	Best For
BFS	Queue	Explores level by level; finds shortest path in unweighted graphs	Finding the shortest path in unweighted graphs

Algorithm	Data Structure Used	Key Feature	Best For
DFS	Stack/Recursion	Explores as deep as possible before backtracking	Exploring entire graph, cycle detection
A (Heuristic)*	Priority Queue	Combines actual cost with estimated cost (heuristic)	Finding the optimal path in weighted graphs

4.4 Data Structures and Storage Strategies

Efficient storage and data management are crucial for handling large graphs, especially when dealing with dynamic or complex systems. This section covers the two primary strategies for storing graph data: in-memory graphs and persistent storage solutions.

In-Memory Graphs

Overview:
In-memory graphs store data in the system's main memory (RAM), providing fast access and rapid processing capabilities. This approach is ideal for scenarios where low latency and high-speed computation are critical.

Key Characteristics:

- **Speed:**
  Access to data stored in RAM is significantly faster compared to disk-based storage.
- **Volatility:**
  Data stored in memory is temporary and lost when the application terminates or the system restarts.
- **Flexibility:**
  In-memory graphs are well-suited for complex computations, real-time analytics, and prototyping.

Common Tools and Libraries:

- **NetworkX:**
  A Python library for creating, manipulating, and analyzing complex networks.
- **Graph-tool:**
  An efficient Python module for graph analysis.

Example: Creating an In-Memory Graph with NetworkX

python

```python
import networkx as nx

# Create an in-memory graph using NetworkX
G = nx.Graph()

# Add nodes with attributes
G.add_node("Agent 1", status="active")
G.add_node("Agent 2", status="idle")
G.add_node("Agent 3", status="active")

# Add edges representing relationships between agents
G.add_edge("Agent 1", "Agent 2", relationship="communicates")
G.add_edge("Agent 2", "Agent 3", relationship="collaborates")

# Access nodes and edges
print("Nodes and their attributes:")
for node, attrs in G.nodes(data=True):
    print(f"{node}: {attrs}")

print("\nEdges and their attributes:")
for u, v, attrs in G.edges(data=True):
    print(f"{u} <-> {v}: {attrs}")
```

Explanation:

- The graph G is created and stored entirely in memory.
- Nodes and edges are added along with custom attributes.
- The script then iterates over the nodes and edges, printing their details.

Persistent Storage Solutions

Overview:
Persistent storage solutions store graph data on disk or in specialized databases, ensuring that the data remains available even after the application terminates. This approach is essential for long-term data retention, large-scale graphs, and distributed systems.

Key Characteristics:

- **Durability:**
  Data is stored permanently and survives system restarts.
- **Scalability:**
  Many persistent storage systems are designed to handle large datasets and can be distributed across multiple servers.
- **Query Capabilities:**
  Graph databases provide powerful query languages (e.g., Cypher for Neo4j) to retrieve and manipulate data efficiently.

Common Technologies:

- **Graph Databases:**
  - **Neo4j:** A popular graph database that uses the Cypher query language.
  - **Amazon Neptune:** A fully managed graph database service.
- **Persistent Key-Value Stores:**
  - **Redis:** Can be used for storing graph-like structures in memory with persistence capabilities.
- **Hybrid Approaches:**
  Some systems combine in-memory processing with persistent storage to balance speed and durability.

Example: Storing and Querying Graph Data with Neo4j

Below is a simplified example using the Neo4j Python driver (assuming Neo4j is installed and running):

python

from neo4j import GraphDatabase

```python
# Define the Neo4j connection details
uri = "bolt://localhost:7687"
username = "neo4j"
password = "your_password"

# Create a driver instance
driver = GraphDatabase.driver(uri, auth=(username, password))

def create_agents_and_relationships(tx):
    # Create nodes and relationships using Cypher queries
    tx.run("CREATE (a:Agent {name: 'Agent 1', status: 'active'})")
    tx.run("CREATE (b:Agent {name: 'Agent 2', status: 'idle'})")
    tx.run("CREATE (c:Agent {name: 'Agent 3', status: 'active'})")
    tx.run("""
        MATCH (a:Agent {name: 'Agent 1'}), (b:Agent {name: 'Agent 2'})
        CREATE (a)-[:COMMUNICATES]->(b)
    """)
    tx.run("""
        MATCH (b:Agent {name: 'Agent 2'}), (c:Agent {name: 'Agent 3'})
        CREATE (b)-[:COLLABORATES]->(c)
    """)

# Open a session and execute the transactions
with driver.session() as session:
    session.write_transaction(create_agents_and_relationships)

print("Graph data stored in Neo4j successfully!")
driver.close()
```

Explanation:

- A connection to the Neo4j database is established using the Bolt protocol.
- Cypher queries are used to create nodes (agents) and relationships.
- The data is stored persistently in the Neo4j database, where it can be queried and updated over time.

Comparison: In-Memory Graphs vs. Persistent Storage Solutions

Aspect	In-Memory Graphs	Persistent Storage Solutions
Speed	Very fast due to RAM access.	Slower compared to RAM, but optimized for disk or distributed storage.
Durability	Volatile; data is lost when the application stops.	Durable; data is retained even after system restarts.
Scalability	Limited by available RAM; best for smaller to medium-sized graphs.	Designed to handle very large datasets; can be distributed across multiple servers.
Use Cases	Real-time analysis, prototyping, simulation.	Long-term storage, enterprise-level applications, large-scale networks.
Query Capabilities	Basic querying using programming languages.	Advanced querying using specialized languages (e.g., Cypher).

In this chapter, we have explored essential graph theory concepts relevant to LangGraph, including basic graph elements, graph traversal, and search algorithms. We discussed BFS, DFS, and heuristic-based A* search, providing detailed explanations and code examples for each. Additionally, we examined data structures and storage strategies for graphs, comparing in-memory approaches with persistent storage solutions.

Understanding these fundamentals enables you to select the appropriate traversal methods and storage strategies based on your system's needs—whether you require rapid, temporary computations or robust, long-term data persistence. This knowledge lays the groundwork for designing, implementing, and optimizing advanced autonomous multi-agent systems using LangGraph.

Chapter 5: Inside the LangGraph Architecture

In this chapter, we delve into the internal workings of LangGraph. We will examine the core components and modules that constitute the LangGraph engine, explore its API layer and integration points, and review the underlying technologies and dependencies that support the framework. This understanding will help you appreciate how LangGraph efficiently manages autonomous multi-agent systems and how you can extend its capabilities to suit your project needs.

5.1 Core Components and Modules

At the heart of LangGraph is a robust engine designed to coordinate multiple autonomous agents and manage their interactions in a dynamic, scalable environment. This section provides an overview of the core components and modules that make up the LangGraph architecture.

The LangGraph Engine and Its Subsystems

The LangGraph engine is a modular framework that is responsible for the following key tasks:

1. **Agent Management:**
   o **Registration and Lifecycle Management:**
     Handles the creation, initialization, and termination of agents. It maintains a registry of active agents and their current states.
   o **Communication Coordination:**
     Manages the message-passing system and event-driven communication between agents, ensuring that messages are correctly routed and delivered.
2. **Task Scheduling and Execution:**
   o **Scheduler:**
     Determines the order and timing for agent actions. It balances load across agents and prioritizes tasks based on system requirements.

- o **Execution Engine:**
  Executes agent actions and processes events in real time. It supports both synchronous and asynchronous processing.
3. **Event Handling and Logging:**
   - o **Event Dispatcher:**
     Listens for events generated by agents or external inputs and routes them to the appropriate handlers.
   - o **Logging and Monitoring:**
     Tracks system events, errors, and performance metrics. This subsystem is essential for debugging and optimizing the overall system.
4. **Error Handling and Recovery:**
   - o **Fault Tolerance:**
     Implements mechanisms to detect, log, and recover from errors or failures. This ensures the system maintains resilience in the face of unexpected issues.
   - o **Self-Healing Capabilities:**
     Automatically restarts or reallocates resources for failed agents to ensure continuous operation.

API Layer and Integration Points

The API layer of LangGraph is designed to expose the core functionalities of the engine to developers, allowing for seamless integration and extension. Key aspects include:

- **Programmatic Access:**
  Developers can interact with LangGraph using a set of well-documented APIs that facilitate the creation, management, and monitoring of agents. This includes methods for:
  - o **Agent Creation:**
    Easily instantiate new agents with specific behaviors.
  - o **Message Passing:**
    Send, receive, and process messages between agents.
  - o **System Query:**
    Retrieve real-time data on agent statuses, event logs, and performance metrics.
- **Plugin Architecture:**
  LangGraph supports a modular plugin system that allows developers to add new features without modifying the core engine. Plugins can enhance functionality in areas such as:

- o **Visualization:**
  Integrate advanced dashboards or third-party visualization libraries.
- o **Communication Protocols:**
  Support additional protocols (e.g., MQTT, WebSockets) to extend agent communication capabilities.
- o **Analytics and Monitoring:**
  Incorporate tools for detailed performance tracking and anomaly detection.
- **Integration with External Services:**
  The API layer also provides integration points with external services and libraries, such as:
  - o **Database Systems:**
    For persistent storage of system data and historical logs.
  - o **Machine Learning Libraries:**
    To enhance agent decision-making through predictive analytics.
  - o **Cloud Services:**
    For deploying LangGraph in scalable, distributed environments.

Example: Extending LangGraph with a Custom Module

Below is a simplified example of how you might create a custom module to extend the functionality of LangGraph. In this example, we define a new module that adds a custom logging mechanism.

python

```python
# custom_logger.py

from langgraph import Module

class CustomLogger(Module):
    """
    A custom logging module that extends LangGraph's logging capabilities.
    """
    def __init__(self, log_file="custom_log.txt"):
        self.log_file = log_file
        super().__init__()

    def log_event(self, event_message):
```

```
"""
    Logs an event message to a specified file.
    """
    with open(self.log_file, "a") as file:
        file.write(event_message + "\n")
    print(f"Logged event: {event_message}")

# Example usage within the LangGraph engine context:
if __name__ == "__main__":
    from langgraph import GraphSystem

    # Create the LangGraph system
    system = GraphSystem()

    # Instantiate and register the custom logger module
    custom_logger = CustomLogger()
    system.register_module(custom_logger)

    # Simulate an event being logged
    custom_logger.log_event("Agent A initialized successfully.")
```

Explanation:

- **Module Inheritance:**
  The CustomLogger class inherits from a generic Module base class
  provided by LangGraph.
- **Custom Functionality:**
  The log_event method writes log messages to a file and prints a
  confirmation message.
- **Integration:**
  The module is registered with the LangGraph system, making its
  functionality available as part of the overall architecture.

5.2 Underlying Technologies and Dependencies

The LangGraph framework is built on a foundation of robust technologies
and libraries that ensure efficiency, scalability, and ease of integration.
Understanding these dependencies helps you appreciate the design choices
behind LangGraph and provides insight into how to extend or customize the
system.

Frameworks and Libraries

LangGraph leverages several popular frameworks and libraries, including:

- **Python:**
  The core programming language used to build LangGraph. Python's simplicity, readability, and rich ecosystem make it an ideal choice for developing complex systems.
- **NetworkX:**
  A comprehensive Python library for creating, manipulating, and analyzing graphs. NetworkX is used extensively in LangGraph for representing agent relationships and performing graph-based computations.
- **Asyncio:**
  Python's asynchronous I/O framework, which is used to handle concurrent operations within LangGraph. Asyncio helps manage non-blocking I/O operations, making the system more responsive and scalable.
- **Flask/Django (Optional):**
  For developers building web interfaces or RESTful APIs to interact with LangGraph, frameworks like Flask or Django can be integrated. These frameworks enable the development of custom dashboards and administrative tools.

Runtime Environments

LangGraph is designed to be flexible in various runtime environments:

- **Local Development:**
  During the development phase, LangGraph runs on a local machine with minimal configuration. This is ideal for prototyping and initial testing.
- **Cloud and Distributed Environments:**
  For production deployments, LangGraph can be deployed on cloud platforms such as AWS, Google Cloud, or Azure. These environments provide scalability, fault tolerance, and managed services that support large-scale multi-agent systems.
- **Containerization:**
  LangGraph supports containerization using Docker. Containers help encapsulate the environment, ensuring consistency across development, testing, and production.

Dependency Management and Installation

Managing dependencies is critical to maintaining a stable and reproducible environment. LangGraph uses standard Python package management practices:

- **Pip and Virtual Environments:**
  Developers are encouraged to use pip along with virtual environments (e.g., venv or conda) to isolate dependencies and avoid conflicts.
- **Requirements File:**
  A requirements.txt file is provided with LangGraph that lists all necessary packages and their versions. This file can be used to set up the environment quickly:

bash

```
pip install -r requirements.txt
```

Example: Inspecting Dependencies

Below is an example of a simplified requirements.txt file for a LangGraph project:

ini

```
# Core dependencies
networkx==2.6.3
asyncio==3.4.3

# Optional dependencies for web interfaces
Flask==2.0.2
gunicorn==20.1.0

# Testing and development
pytest==6.2.5
```

Explanation:

- **Core Dependencies:**
  networkx and asyncio are essential for graph operations and asynchronous processing.

- **Optional Dependencies:**
  Flask and Gunicorn may be used if you decide to build a web-based dashboard or API.
- **Testing:**
  Pytest is included to facilitate unit testing and ensure code quality.

Integration Points and Extensibility

LangGraph is designed to be highly extensible. Its modular architecture and API layer allow you to integrate with various external systems and libraries. Common integration points include:

- **External Databases:**
  Connect to SQL or NoSQL databases for persistent storage.
- **Machine Learning Frameworks:**
  Integrate with libraries such as TensorFlow or PyTorch to add intelligent decision-making capabilities.
- **Monitoring and Analytics:**
  Use tools like Prometheus and Grafana to monitor system performance and visualize key metrics.

In this chapter, we explored the inner workings of LangGraph by examining its core components and modules, as well as the underlying technologies and dependencies that support the framework. The LangGraph engine, with its modular architecture, robust API layer, and extensible plugin system, provides a powerful platform for building and managing autonomous multi-agent systems.

Understanding these architectural details not only helps in using LangGraph effectively but also empowers you to extend its functionality to meet specific requirements. Whether you are integrating external services, customizing modules, or deploying the system in a distributed environment, the insights provided in this chapter serve as a solid foundation for advanced development and optimization.

5.3 Extensibility: Plugins and Custom Modules

LangGraph is built with extensibility in mind, allowing you to tailor the framework to meet the unique requirements of your projects. By supporting plugins and custom modules, LangGraph enables you to add new features, integrate external systems, or modify existing behaviors without altering the core engine. This section explains how to extend LangGraph's functionality through its plugin architecture and custom modules.

Extending LangGraph's Functionality

Plugin Architecture Overview

LangGraph's plugin architecture is designed to be modular and loosely coupled. This means you can add or remove plugins with minimal impact on the rest of the system. Key characteristics of the plugin architecture include:

- **Modularity:**
  Each plugin functions as an independent module that can be loaded, unloaded, or updated without affecting other parts of the system.
- **Loose Coupling:**
  Plugins interact with LangGraph through well-defined APIs, ensuring that changes in the core system do not break plugin functionality.
- **Dynamic Loading:**
  Plugins can be discovered and loaded at runtime, allowing for a flexible and adaptive system that can incorporate new capabilities on the fly.

Creating Custom Modules

Custom modules allow you to extend the functionality of LangGraph beyond the standard offerings. Whether you need to implement a new communication protocol, add a specialized data processing algorithm, or integrate with an external service, custom modules provide the necessary framework.

Steps to Develop a Plugin or Custom Module

1. **Define the Module Interface:**
   LangGraph provides a base class or interface that all modules should extend. This interface defines essential methods that your module must implement. For example, a logging module might need to implement methods like initialize(), process_event(), and shutdown().
2. **Implement the Module:**
   Write your module by extending the base class and implementing the

required functionality. Ensure your code is modular and follows LangGraph's coding conventions.

3. **Register the Module with LangGraph:**
   Once your module is implemented, you must register it with the LangGraph system. Registration makes your module's services available to the entire framework.

4. **Test and Debug:**
   Rigorously test your module to ensure it integrates seamlessly with LangGraph. Use unit tests and real-world scenarios to validate its behavior.

Example: Creating a Custom Analytics Plugin

Below is an example that demonstrates how to create a custom analytics plugin that calculates and logs the average response time of agents.

python

```python
# custom_analytics.py

from langgraph import Module

class CustomAnalytics(Module):
    """
    A custom analytics plugin that calculates the average response time
    of agents and logs the results.
    """
    def __init__(self):
        self.response_times = []
        super().__init__()

    def initialize(self):
        """
        Called when the module is registered with the LangGraph system.
        Initialize any required variables or connections here.
        """
        print("CustomAnalytics module initialized.")

    def record_response_time(self, response_time):
        """
        Record an agent's response time.
        """
```

```python
        self.response_times.append(response_time)
        print(f"Recorded response time: {response_time}ms")

    def calculate_average_response_time(self):
        """
        Calculate and return the average response time of all recorded values.
        """
        if self.response_times:
            average = sum(self.response_times) / len(self.response_times)
            print(f"Average Response Time: {average:.2f}ms")
            return average
        else:
            print("No response times recorded yet.")
            return None

    def shutdown(self):
        """
        Clean up any resources if necessary before the module is unloaded.
        """
        print("CustomAnalytics module shutting down.")

# Example usage within the LangGraph engine context:
if __name__ == "__main__":
    from langgraph import GraphSystem

    # Create the LangGraph system
    system = GraphSystem()

    # Instantiate and register the custom analytics plugin
    analytics_plugin = CustomAnalytics()
    system.register_module(analytics_plugin)

    # Simulate recording response times from agents
    analytics_plugin.record_response_time(120)
    analytics_plugin.record_response_time(150)
    analytics_plugin.record_response_time(100)

    # Calculate and display the average response time
    analytics_plugin.calculate_average_response_time()
```

Explanation:

- **Module Inheritance:**
  The CustomAnalytics class extends the Module base class provided by LangGraph.
- **Lifecycle Methods:**
  The module implements initialize() and shutdown() to manage its lifecycle.
- **Core Functionality:**
  The record_response_time() method collects response times, while calculate_average_response_time() computes and logs the average.
- **Integration:**
  The module is registered with the LangGraph system using system.register_module(analytics_plugin), making its functions available for use throughout the system.

Summary Table: Extensibility Features

Feature	Description	Benefit
Modularity	Plugins function as independent modules.	Easy to add, remove, or update functionalities.
Loose Coupling	Interacts through well-defined APIs.	Minimizes dependency issues and core system impact.
Dynamic Loading	Plugins are loaded at runtime.	Enhances system flexibility and adaptability.
Custom Modules	Extend functionality beyond default capabilities.	Tailor the system to specific project requirements.

5.4 Security, Robustness, and Data Integrity

Ensuring the security, robustness, and data integrity of a multi-agent system is critical, especially when these systems operate in dynamic, distributed environments. LangGraph incorporates several mechanisms to protect the system and maintain its reliability.

Security Mechanisms

Authentication and Authorization

- **Authentication:**
  Verify the identity of agents and users interacting with the system. LangGraph supports token-based authentication or integration with external identity providers (e.g., OAuth, LDAP).
- **Authorization:**
  Define access control policies to ensure that agents can only perform actions they are permitted to. This can involve role-based access control (RBAC) or attribute-based access control (ABAC).

Data Encryption

- **In-Transit Encryption:**
  Use secure communication protocols (e.g., TLS/SSL) to protect data as it moves between agents and external services.
- **At-Rest Encryption:**
  Encrypt sensitive data stored in memory, files, or databases to prevent unauthorized access in the event of a security breach.

Secure Coding Practices

- **Input Validation:**
  Validate all external inputs to prevent injection attacks or malformed data from compromising the system.
- **Regular Security Audits:**
  Periodically review and update the codebase to address potential vulnerabilities.

Robustness Mechanisms

Fault Tolerance and Error Handling

- **Redundancy:**
  Implement redundant components (e.g., backup agents or servers) to ensure that the failure of one component does not cause a system-wide outage.
- **Failover Strategies:**
  Automatically detect failures and switch to standby components or backup processes to maintain system continuity.

- **Exception Handling:**
  Incorporate robust error handling in code to gracefully manage unexpected events without crashing the system.

Self-Healing Capabilities

- **Automated Recovery:**
  LangGraph can monitor the health of its agents and automatically restart or reassign tasks when issues are detected.
- **Resource Reallocation:**
  Dynamically allocate resources (e.g., CPU, memory) to ensure optimal performance even under load or during failures.

Data Integrity Mechanisms

Consistency and Verification

- **Transaction Management:**
  Ensure that changes to the system state occur as atomic transactions. This means that either all operations in a transaction succeed, or none do, preventing partial updates.
- **Checksums and Hashing:**
  Use cryptographic hash functions or checksums to verify that data has not been tampered with or corrupted during transmission or storage.

Logging and Auditing

- **Event Logging:**
  Maintain comprehensive logs of all system events, including errors, agent actions, and data modifications. Logs are essential for forensic analysis and auditing.
- **Audit Trails:**
  Implement audit trails that record who accessed or modified data, ensuring accountability and traceability in the system.

Example: Implementing Basic Security and Robustness in LangGraph

Below is a simple example demonstrating how you might incorporate error handling and logging to improve the robustness of a LangGraph agent module.

python

```python
# secure_module.py

from langgraph import Module

class SecureAgentModule(Module):
    """
    A module that demonstrates basic security and robustness features.
    """

    def __init__(self):
        super().__init__()
        self.event_log = []

    def process_event(self, event):
        """
        Process an event with basic error handling and logging.
        """
        try:
            # Validate event structure
            if not isinstance(event, dict) or "type" not in event:
                raise ValueError("Invalid event structure")

            # Simulate event processing based on type
            if event["type"] == "data_update":
                self._update_data(event["data"])
            else:
                print(f"Unhandled event type: {event['type']}")

            # Log the successful processing of the event
            self._log_event(f"Successfully processed event: {event}")

        except Exception as e:
            # Log the error with details
            error_message = f"Error processing event: {event} | Error: {str(e)}"
            self._log_event(error_message)
```

```python
        print(error_message)

    def _update_data(self, data):
        """
        A placeholder method to simulate data update.
        """
        # Here you would include code to update data safely, ensuring
transaction integrity
        print(f"Data updated to: {data}")

    def _log_event(self, message):
        """
        Log an event message to the module's internal log.
        """
        self.event_log.append(message)
        # In a real-world scenario, you might also write this to a secure log file
or external logging service
        print(f"Log: {message}")

# Example usage:
if __name__ == "__main__":
    secure_module = SecureAgentModule()

    # Process a valid event
    event_valid = {"type": "data_update", "data": "New Value"}
    secure_module.process_event(event_valid)

    # Process an invalid event to trigger error handling
    event_invalid = "Invalid event format"
    secure_module.process_event(event_invalid)
```

Explanation:

- **Event Validation:**
  The process_event method checks if the event is a dictionary and
  contains the required "type" key. If not, it raises an error.
- **Error Handling:**
  The method uses a try-except block to catch and log exceptions,
  ensuring that errors do not crash the system.
- **Logging:**
  The _log_event method records messages to an internal event log and

prints them. In practice, these logs could be forwarded to a centralized logging system.

- **Data Update Placeholder:**
  The _update_data method simulates a data update, where you would implement transaction management and data integrity checks.

Summary Table: Security, Robustness, and Data Integrity

Aspect	Mechanism	Description	Benefit
Authentication	Token-based, OAuth, LDAP	Verifies the identity of agents and users.	Prevents unauthorized access.
Authorization	Role-based/Attribute-based	Controls what actions authenticated entities can perform.	Limits access to sensitive functions.
Encryption	TLS/SSL (in-transit), AES (at-rest)	Protects data during transmission and storage.	Ensures confidentiality and prevents tampering.
Error Handling	Exception handling, failover strategies	Catches errors and switches to backup components automatically.	Maintains system stability under failure.
Logging and Auditing	Event logs, audit trails	Records system events and changes to data.	Enhances accountability and aids in forensic analysis.
Data Verification	Checksums, hash functions	Verifies data integrity during operations.	Prevents corruption and ensures consistency.

In this section, we explored how LangGraph's extensibility features allow you to tailor the framework through plugins and custom modules. We demonstrated how to create a custom analytics plugin and discussed the benefits of modularity, loose coupling, and dynamic loading. We then addressed security, robustness, and data integrity by outlining key mechanisms such as authentication, encryption, fault tolerance, self-healing, and comprehensive logging.

By incorporating these practices, you can build multi-agent systems that are not only feature-rich and extensible but also secure, reliable, and resilient in the face of challenges. This ensures that your LangGraph-based applications can operate effectively in diverse and demanding environments.

Chapter 6: Designing Your Multi-Agent System

Designing an effective multi-agent system (MAS) requires careful planning and a deep understanding of both your problem domain and the objectives you wish to achieve. In this chapter, we will explore two essential aspects of system design: gathering requirements and planning the system, and modeling the problem domain using graphs. By following these steps, you can ensure that your system is well-defined, scalable, and capable of meeting your project goals.

6.1 Requirements Gathering and System Planning

Before diving into the technical implementation of your multi-agent system with LangGraph, it is crucial to define the objectives and success criteria that will drive your project. This process involves gathering detailed requirements and planning the overall system architecture.

Defining Objectives

Objectives are the high-level goals that your system must achieve. They guide the design process and help prioritize features and functionalities. When defining your objectives, consider the following:

- **Purpose of the System:**
  What problem does your system aim to solve? For example, is it designed for real-time decision making in an industrial setting, for efficient resource allocation, or for automating routine tasks in a smart city?
- **User Needs and Stakeholder Expectations:**
  Identify the end users and stakeholders. What are their expectations? What features will deliver the most value? In a multi-agent system, stakeholders might include system administrators, operators, or even other integrated systems.
- **Performance Metrics:**
  Determine the key performance indicators (KPIs) that will measure the success of your system. Common metrics include response time, throughput, reliability, and scalability.

- **Operational Environment:**
  Consider the context in which your system will operate. Will it run on a local network, in the cloud, or in a distributed environment? What are the constraints (e.g., hardware, network latency) that need to be addressed?

Success Criteria

Success criteria are specific, measurable outcomes that define when your system has met its objectives. They provide a clear basis for evaluating the system's performance. Here are some examples of success criteria for a multi-agent system:

- **Functionality:**
  The system should support the dynamic creation, modification, and termination of agents, and provide seamless communication between them.
- **Scalability:**
  The system must handle an increasing number of agents and interactions without a significant drop in performance. For example, it should maintain response times under a specified threshold even as the agent count grows.
- **Reliability:**
  The system should exhibit high uptime and be resilient to failures. This may involve a defined percentage of successful transactions or minimal downtime over a set period.
- **User Satisfaction:**
  If applicable, user feedback should indicate that the system is intuitive, efficient, and meets the needs of its intended audience.

Requirements Gathering Process

The process of gathering requirements can be broken down into several steps:

1. **Stakeholder Interviews and Workshops:**
   Engage with stakeholders to capture their vision, needs, and expectations. Document these insights carefully.
2. **Use Case Development:**
   Develop detailed use cases that illustrate how the system will be used in real-world scenarios. This helps in understanding the interactions and workflows that need to be supported.

3. **Feasibility Study:**
   Evaluate the technical and operational feasibility of the proposed system. This includes assessing available resources, potential risks, and cost-benefit analyses.
4. **Documentation:**
   Create a comprehensive requirements document that includes objectives, success criteria, use cases, and any constraints or assumptions. This document serves as a reference point throughout the development process.

Example: Requirements Table

Below is an example of a requirements table that captures some key objectives and success criteria for a hypothetical multi-agent system designed for resource management in a smart building.

Objective	Description	Success Criteria
Efficient Resource Allocation	Automatically manage energy usage and optimize HVAC systems.	Achieve at least a 15% reduction in energy consumption.
Real-Time Monitoring	Provide continuous monitoring of system performance and environmental data.	System latency under 200ms for real-time alerts.
Scalability	Support the dynamic addition of new sensors and control agents.	Handle a 100% increase in agents with no more than 10% performance degradation.
User-Friendly Interface	Offer an intuitive dashboard for facility managers to monitor operations.	Positive user feedback from at least 80% of users in surveys.

6.2 Modeling the Problem Domain Using Graphs

Once the requirements are clearly defined, the next step is to model your problem domain. In the context of LangGraph, graph modeling provides a powerful method for representing agents, their interactions, and the overall workflows of your system.

Identifying Agents

Start by identifying the individual components or entities that will act as autonomous agents in your system. Consider the following:

- **Types of Agents:**
  Determine the different roles agents will play. For example, in a smart building, agents might include temperature sensors, HVAC controllers, occupancy sensors, and security systems.
- **Agent Attributes:**
  Define the characteristics and attributes for each agent type. This may include identifiers, status, location, capabilities, and operational parameters.
- **Agent Relationships:**
  Identify how agents interact with one another. Do they exchange messages directly, collaborate on tasks, or depend on one another's data? This will form the basis of the graph's edges.

Mapping Interactions and Workflows

Once the agents are identified, model the interactions and workflows between them using graph elements:

- **Nodes Represent Agents:**
  Each agent is represented as a node in the graph. Include attributes such as name, type, and status as node properties.
- **Edges Represent Interactions:**
  Interactions such as communication, data sharing, or task coordination are modeled as edges connecting the nodes. Edges may have attributes such as the type of interaction or frequency.
- **Workflows as Graph Paths:**
  Workflows—sequences of interactions that accomplish specific tasks—can be modeled as paths through the graph. This helps in visualizing and optimizing the overall process.

Example: Graph Modeling of a Smart Building System

Consider a simplified smart building system where various agents collaborate to manage energy usage. Here's how you might model this system:

1. **Agents Identified:**

- o **Temperature Sensors:** Measure the temperature in different zones.
- o **HVAC Controllers:** Adjust heating, ventilation, and air conditioning based on sensor data.
- o **Occupancy Sensors:** Detect the presence of people in various areas.
- o **Energy Management System (EMS):** Central controller that oversees energy distribution.

2. **Interactions Mapped:**
   - o Temperature sensors send data to HVAC controllers.
   - o Occupancy sensors notify both HVAC controllers and the EMS.
   - o The EMS monitors overall system performance and can send override commands to HVAC controllers.

Example Code: Modeling a System Using NetworkX

Below is a code example that uses Python's NetworkX library to model the smart building system as a graph.

python

```
import networkx as nx
import matplotlib.pyplot as plt

# Create a graph to model the smart building system
smart_building_graph = nx.DiGraph()  # Directed graph, since interactions
have a direction

# Add nodes representing agents with attributes
agents = [
    ("TempSensor_1", {"type": "Temperature Sensor", "zone": "Lobby"}),
    ("TempSensor_2", {"type": "Temperature Sensor", "zone": "Conference
Room"}),
    ("HVAC_Controller_1", {"type": "HVAC Controller", "zone": "Lobby"}),
    ("HVAC_Controller_2", {"type": "HVAC Controller", "zone":
"Conference Room"}),
    ("OccupancySensor_1", {"type": "Occupancy Sensor", "zone": "Lobby"}),
    ("EMS", {"type": "Energy Management System"})
]

for agent, attrs in agents:
```

```python
    smart_building_graph.add_node(agent, **attrs)

# Add edges representing interactions between agents
edges = [
    ("TempSensor_1", "HVAC_Controller_1", {"interaction": "sends
temperature data"}),
    ("TempSensor_2", "HVAC_Controller_2", {"interaction": "sends
temperature data"}),
    ("OccupancySensor_1", "HVAC_Controller_1", {"interaction": "sends
occupancy data"}),
    ("OccupancySensor_1", "EMS", {"interaction": "reports occupancy"}),
    ("HVAC_Controller_1", "EMS", {"interaction": "reports energy usage"}),
    ("HVAC_Controller_2", "EMS", {"interaction": "reports energy usage"}),
    ("EMS", "HVAC_Controller_1", {"interaction": "sends override
command"}),
    ("EMS", "HVAC_Controller_2", {"interaction": "sends override
command"})
]

for source, target, attrs in edges:
    smart_building_graph.add_edge(source, target, **attrs)

# Visualize the graph
plt.figure(figsize=(10, 8))
pos = nx.spring_layout(smart_building_graph)
nx.draw(smart_building_graph, pos, with_labels=True,
node_color='lightblue', edge_color='gray', node_size=2000, font_size=10)

# Draw edge labels to show interaction types
edge_labels = nx.get_edge_attributes(smart_building_graph, 'interaction')
nx.draw_networkx_edge_labels(smart_building_graph, pos,
edge_labels=edge_labels, font_color='red')

plt.title("Smart Building Multi-Agent System")
plt.show()
```

Explanation:

- **Graph Initialization:**
  A directed graph (DiGraph) is used to represent the system, capturing
  the direction of interactions.

- **Adding Nodes:**
  Agents are added as nodes with attributes such as type and zone. This information helps in identifying the role of each agent within the system.
- **Adding Edges:**
  Edges are added to represent interactions between agents. Each edge includes an attribute that describes the nature of the interaction (e.g., sending data, reporting, or commanding).
- **Visualization:**
  The graph is visualized using a spring layout, with edge labels indicating the types of interactions. This visualization helps stakeholders quickly understand the workflow and dependencies within the system.

Summary Table: Modeling the Problem Domain

Component	Graph Element	Description	Example
Agent	Node	Represents an autonomous entity with attributes (e.g., type, zone)	Temperature Sensor, HVAC Controller, EMS
Interaction	Edge	Represents communication or dependency between agents	"Sends temperature data", "Reports energy usage"
Workflow	Graph Path	Sequence of interactions that accomplish a specific task	Sensor data flowing to controllers and then to EMS

Designing your multi-agent system involves a clear understanding of the system's objectives, success criteria, and operational requirements, followed by an accurate modeling of the problem domain. In this chapter, we explored how to gather requirements and plan your system by defining clear objectives and measurable success criteria. We then demonstrated how to model the problem domain using graphs, identifying the agents, their interactions, and the workflows that tie everything together.

By following these detailed and structured approaches, you create a solid foundation for building, implementing, and scaling an efficient multi-agent system using LangGraph. This planning and modeling phase ensures that your system is well-aligned with stakeholder expectations and is capable of adapting to the dynamic challenges of real-world applications.

6.3 Architectural Patterns for Multi-Agent Systems

When designing a multi-agent system (MAS), one of the critical decisions is selecting the appropriate architectural pattern. The architecture dictates how agents interact, share information, and achieve overall system objectives. In this section, we will discuss three primary architectural patterns: centralized, decentralized, and hybrid models. Each pattern offers distinct benefits and trade-offs, and the choice largely depends on the application requirements, system scale, and desired performance characteristics.

Centralized Architecture

Overview

In a centralized architecture, a single central entity (often called a central coordinator or master agent) is responsible for managing the overall system. This central node typically handles tasks such as decision-making, data aggregation, and control functions. All agents communicate directly with this central authority rather than with each other.

Key Characteristics

- **Control and Coordination:**
  The central coordinator oversees system behavior, making it easier to enforce uniform policies and decisions.
- **Simplified Communication:**
  Agents send data to and receive commands from a central node, reducing the complexity of direct peer-to-peer interactions.
- **Easier Debugging and Management:**
  Since one component controls the system, monitoring, and maintaining the system can be more straightforward.

Trade-Offs

- **Scalability Limitations:**
  As the number of agents increases, the central coordinator may become a bottleneck.

- **Single Point of Failure:**
  If the central node fails, the entire system's functionality can be compromised.

Example Scenario

A centralized architecture might be appropriate for a small-scale smart building system where a central controller manages lighting, HVAC, and security systems.

Diagram Illustration

pgsql

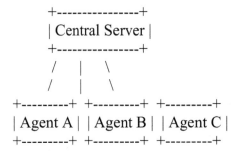

```
        +----------------+
        | Central Server |
        +----------------+
         /    |    \
        /     |     \
+---------+ +---------+ +---------+
| Agent A | | Agent B | | Agent C |
+---------+ +---------+ +---------+
```

Decentralized Architecture

Overview

In a decentralized architecture, control and decision-making are distributed among the agents themselves. There is no single point of control; instead, agents communicate directly with one another and collectively determine actions through local interactions.

Key Characteristics

- **High Scalability:**
  Since no central coordinator is required, the system can scale more easily to accommodate a large number of agents.
- **Robustness and Fault Tolerance:**
  The absence of a single point of failure makes the system more resilient; if one agent fails, others can continue to operate.

- **Flexible and Adaptive:**
  Agents can dynamically form groups, reassign tasks, and adapt to changes in the environment.

Trade-Offs

- **Complex Coordination:**
  Achieving consensus or coordinated action among a large number of autonomous agents can be challenging.
- **Increased Communication Overhead:**
  Peer-to-peer communication can lead to more complex and possibly redundant message exchanges.

Example Scenario

A decentralized architecture might be used in swarm robotics, where each robot makes decisions based on local sensor data and communicates with its neighbors to collectively achieve tasks like area coverage or obstacle avoidance.

Diagram Illustration

lua

```
+---------+      +---------+
| Agent A |-------| Agent B |
+---------+      +---------+
     \        /
      \      /
    +---------+
    | Agent C |
    +---------+
```

Hybrid Architecture

Overview

A hybrid architecture combines elements of both centralized and decentralized systems. In a hybrid model, a central coordinator may exist for high-level decision-making and coordination, while individual agents retain autonomy for local decisions and operations.

Key Characteristics

- **Balanced Control:**
  Centralized functions manage overall system strategy and resource allocation, while decentralized components handle local, real-time interactions.
- **Improved Scalability and Resilience:**
  By delegating routine tasks to autonomous agents, the central coordinator is relieved of some load, reducing the risk of bottlenecks.
- **Enhanced Flexibility:**
  The system can adapt to both global changes (via the central node) and local variations (through decentralized control).

Trade-Offs

- **System Complexity:**
  Combining centralized and decentralized elements can increase the overall complexity of system design and integration.
- **Coordination Challenges:**
  Ensuring smooth interaction between centralized control and autonomous agents requires well-designed communication protocols and interfaces.

Example Scenario

A hybrid system might be deployed in a smart city environment, where a central system monitors overall traffic and energy usage, while individual traffic lights and sensors operate autonomously to manage local conditions.

Diagram Illustration

sql

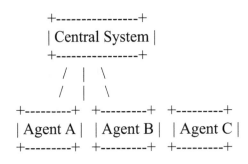

```
        +----------------+
        | Central System |
        +----------------+
           /   |   \
          /    |    \
  +---------+  +---------+  +---------+
  | Agent A |  | Agent B |  | Agent C |
  +---------+  +---------+  +---------+
```

Comparison Summary Table

Aspect	Centralized	Decentralized	Hybrid
Control	Single central coordinator	Distributed among agents	Combination of central and local control
Scalability	Limited by central node capacity	High scalability, no central bottleneck	Scalable through delegation and balance
Fault Tolerance	Vulnerable to central node failure	Resilient, no single point of failure	Enhanced resilience with fallback mechanisms
Communication Complexity	Simpler, direct communication with central node	Complex, many peer-to-peer interactions	Moderate, balanced between central and local
Use Cases	Small to medium systems, tightly controlled environments	Large-scale, distributed systems	Systems requiring both global oversight and local autonomy

6.4 Toolsets and Methodologies for System Design

Successful design and development of a multi-agent system involve not only selecting the right architecture but also using appropriate tools and methodologies. This section outlines various toolsets and design methodologies that facilitate system planning, prototyping, documentation, and simulation.

Design Documentation

Importance

Design documentation serves as the blueprint for your multi-agent system. It captures requirements, architectural decisions, workflows, and interactions, ensuring that all stakeholders have a common understanding of the system.

Components of Design Documentation

- **System Requirements:**
  Detailed descriptions of functional and non-functional requirements.
- **Architecture Diagrams:**
  Visual representations of system components, interactions, and data flows.
- **Use Case Descriptions:**
  Scenarios that illustrate how the system will be used in practice.
- **Technical Specifications:**
  Detailed technical descriptions, including API interfaces, data models, and protocols.

Tools for Documentation

- **UML Tools:**
  Tools such as Lucidchart, Microsoft Visio, or draw.io can be used to create UML diagrams, flowcharts, and other visual representations.
- **Markdown/LaTeX:**
  For text-based documentation, Markdown or LaTeX is widely used, especially when integrated with version control systems like Git.
- **Confluence/Notion:**
  These platforms allow for collaborative documentation, making it easier for teams to contribute and maintain updated design documents.

Prototyping and Simulation

Purpose

Prototyping and simulation allow you to validate your system design and assess its performance under various scenarios before full-scale implementation. These methods help in identifying potential issues early, reducing risks, and refining system behavior.

Prototyping Methodologies

- **Rapid Prototyping:**
  Develop a minimal viable version of your system to test core

functionalities. This can be done using frameworks like LangGraph to quickly assemble a working model.

- **Iterative Development:**
  Build the system in small increments, testing and refining each component before moving on to the next phase. This agile approach allows for continuous improvement based on feedback.

Simulation Tools

- **Network Simulators:**
  Tools like NS-3 or OMNeT++ can simulate networked environments and interactions between agents.
- **Custom Simulation Frameworks:**
  Use Python libraries (such as SimPy) to create custom simulations that model agent behaviors, interactions, and system dynamics.
- **Visualization Tools:**
  Tools like Matplotlib, Plotly, or Gephi can help visualize simulation results and agent interactions, providing insights into system performance.

Example: Rapid Prototyping with LangGraph

Below is a simple example demonstrating rapid prototyping of a multi-agent system using LangGraph. In this prototype, we create a minimal system with a few agents to test basic communication and coordination.

python

```
# rapid_prototype.py

from langgraph import GraphSystem, Agent

# Define a simple agent that prints a message upon receiving communication
class PrototypeAgent(Agent):
    def __init__(self, name):
        super().__init__(name)

    def act(self):
        print(f"{self.name} is active and processing tasks.")

# Create a prototype LangGraph system
prototype_system = GraphSystem()
```

```
# Instantiate a few prototype agents
agent1 = PrototypeAgent("Agent 1")
agent2 = PrototypeAgent("Agent 2")
agent3 = PrototypeAgent("Agent 3")

# Register agents with the system
prototype_system.add_agent(agent1)
prototype_system.add_agent(agent2)
prototype_system.add_agent(agent3)

# Simulate basic agent actions
agent1.act()
agent2.act()
agent3.act()
```

Explanation:

- **Agent Definition:**
  The PrototypeAgent class is a simple extension of the LangGraph
  Agent class, where the act() method is defined to print a status
  message.
- **System Setup:**
  A minimal LangGraph system is created, and several prototype
  agents are added to it.
- **Simulation Execution:**
  The agents execute their actions, demonstrating basic functionality
  and communication. This prototype can be expanded iteratively to
  include more complex behaviors and interactions.

Methodologies for System Design

Agile and Iterative Development

Agile methodologies emphasize iterative development, continuous feedback,
and flexibility. By developing your multi-agent system in small, manageable
increments, you can adapt to changing requirements and improve system
performance based on real-world testing.

Design Thinking

Design thinking is a user-centric approach that focuses on understanding user needs, brainstorming innovative solutions, prototyping, and testing. In the context of multi-agent systems, design thinking can help ensure that the system is not only technically robust but also aligned with user and stakeholder expectations.

Model-Driven Engineering (MDE)

MDE involves creating abstract models of the system that can be automatically transformed into executable code. This methodology is particularly useful for complex systems, as it promotes consistency and reduces manual coding errors. Graph-based models in LangGraph naturally lend themselves to MDE practices.

Comparison Summary Table

Aspect	Documentation Tools	Prototyping & Simulation Tools	Methodologies
Purpose	Capture requirements and design details	Validate system design and performance	Facilitate iterative development and innovation
Examples	Lucidchart, Markdown, Confluence	NS-3, OMNeT++, SimPy, Matplotlib, Plotly, Gephi	Agile, Design Thinking, Model-Driven Engineering
Benefits	Clear, accessible, and updated design records	Early detection of issues, performance insights	Adaptability, user-centered design, reduced errors

Architectural patterns and robust toolsets form the backbone of a successful multi-agent system design. In this section, we examined three architectural patterns—centralized, decentralized, and hybrid—highlighting their characteristics, advantages, and trade-offs. We then explored various toolsets and methodologies that support effective system design, including design documentation, prototyping, simulation, and iterative development approaches.

By leveraging these patterns and tools, you can design a multi-agent system that is not only aligned with stakeholder requirements and success criteria but also scalable, resilient, and adaptable to changing environments. This comprehensive approach to design ensures that your LangGraph-based system will be well-prepared to meet the challenges of real-world applications.

Chapter 7: Implementing Autonomous Agents in LangGraph

Implementing autonomous agents in LangGraph involves a systematic approach that spans the entire development lifecycle—from initial design to final deployment. In this chapter, we will explore the stages involved in creating effective agents and discuss coding best practices to ensure your agents are efficient, maintainable, and scalable.

7.1 Agent Development Lifecycle

The agent development lifecycle encompasses four primary phases: design, development, testing, and deployment. Each phase plays a critical role in ensuring that agents behave as expected and integrate seamlessly within the LangGraph framework.

Phases of the Agent Development Lifecycle

Below is an overview table summarizing each phase:

Phase	Description	Key Activities
Design	Plan the agent's behavior, interactions, and integration within the system.	Define objectives, create flowcharts, design interfaces, model interactions.
Development	Write the agent code, integrating LangGraph APIs and implementing defined behaviors.	Code implementation, module creation, integration of external libraries.
Testing	Verify that the agent behaves correctly under various scenarios and meets performance requirements.	Unit testing, integration testing, simulation of real-world scenarios.
Deployment	Release the agent into the production environment and monitor its	Environment setup, continuous integration/continuous deployment (CI/CD), monitoring.

Phase	Description	Key Activities
	performance for continuous improvement.	

1. Design Phase

In the design phase, you lay the foundation for your agent by determining what problem it will solve and how it will interact with other system components. Key steps include:

- **Defining Objectives:**
  Identify the specific tasks the agent will perform and establish measurable success criteria.
- **Modeling Interactions:**
  Use diagrams or graph-based models to map out how the agent will communicate with other agents and components. For instance, in a multi-agent system, you might create a flowchart to illustrate message passing, event handling, and decision-making processes.
- **Interface Design:**
  Plan the API and data exchange formats that your agent will use to interact with LangGraph. This step ensures that the agent's communication is standardized and consistent with the rest of the system.

2. Development Phase

During development, you translate your design into working code. LangGraph provides an API that simplifies agent creation and management. Below is a simple code example that demonstrates the creation of an autonomous agent using LangGraph.

Example: Basic Autonomous Agent

python

```
# basic_agent.py

from langgraph import Agent

class BasicAgent(Agent):
    """
```

A basic autonomous agent that demonstrates essential behaviors.
"""
```python
def __init__(self, name):
    # Initialize the base Agent with a name
    super().__init__(name)
    # Initialize any additional attributes here
    self.task_count = 0

def act(self):
    """
    The primary action of the agent.
    """
    self.task_count += 1
    print(f"{self.name} is performing task #{self.task_count}")

def receive_message(self, message, sender):
    """
    Handle incoming messages.
    """
    print(f"{self.name} received message from {sender.name}: {message}")

# Example usage:
if __name__ == "__main__":
    # Create an instance of BasicAgent
    agent = BasicAgent("Agent Alpha")
    # Simulate the agent performing its action
    agent.act()
    # Simulate receiving a message
    agent.receive_message("Hello, Agent!", agent)
```

Explanation:

- **Class Definition:**
  The BasicAgent class extends the LangGraph Agent class. It defines its own attributes, such as task_count, to track how many tasks have been performed.
- **Method Implementation:**
  The act() method simulates the agent performing a task, and the receive_message() method handles incoming messages. These methods represent typical behaviors in an autonomous agent.

3. Testing Phase

Testing is crucial to validate the behavior and reliability of your agents.
Testing can be performed at multiple levels:

- **Unit Testing:**
  Test individual methods or functions to ensure they work as intended.
  Use frameworks like pytest to automate your unit tests.
- **Integration Testing:**
  Validate that the agent interacts correctly with the LangGraph
  framework and other agents. This can involve simulating message
  exchanges and event handling in a controlled environment.
- **Simulation:**
  Run simulations to assess how your agents behave under realistic
  conditions. This is particularly important in systems where agents
  must respond to dynamic changes in their environment.

Example: Simple Unit Test Using Pytest

python

```
# test_basic_agent.py

import pytest
from basic_agent import BasicAgent

def test_agent_task_count():
    agent = BasicAgent("Test Agent")
    # Initially, task_count should be 0
    assert agent.task_count == 0
    # Perform an action and check if task_count increments
    agent.act()
    assert agent.task_count == 1

def test_receive_message(capsys):
    agent = BasicAgent("Test Agent")
    # Simulate receiving a message
    agent.receive_message("Test Message", agent)
    # Capture the output
    captured = capsys.readouterr().out
    assert "Test Agent received message" in captured
```

```python
if __name__ == "__main__":
    pytest.main()
```

Explanation:

- **Test Functions:**
  Two test functions are defined. The first tests that the task_count increments when act() is called, and the second checks that the receive_message() function produces the expected output.
- **Pytest Framework:**
  The tests are designed to be run with the pytest framework, providing automated validation of the agent's functionality.

4. Deployment Phase

Deployment involves moving your tested agents from a development environment to production. This phase includes:

- **Environment Setup:**
  Configure the production environment, ensuring all dependencies and configurations match the testing setup.
- **Continuous Integration/Continuous Deployment (CI/CD):**
  Implement CI/CD pipelines to automate the deployment process and facilitate rapid updates.
- **Monitoring and Maintenance:**
  Once deployed, continuously monitor agent performance, logs, and system metrics to quickly detect and resolve issues.

Example: Simple Deployment Script

bash

```bash
#!/bin/bash
# deploy.sh - A simple deployment script for LangGraph agents

# Activate the virtual environment
source env/bin/activate

# Install dependencies
pip install -r requirements.txt

# Run tests to ensure everything is working
```

```
pytest

# Start the LangGraph system
python run_langgraph.py

echo "Deployment complete. LangGraph system is now running."
```

Explanation:

- **Script Steps:**
  The script activates a virtual environment, installs dependencies, runs tests, and then starts the LangGraph system. This ensures that only validated code is deployed.
- **Automation:**
  Automating the deployment process minimizes human error and ensures consistency across environments.

7.2 Coding Best Practices for Agent Behavior

Writing maintainable and efficient code is essential for the long-term success of your multi-agent system. In this section, we discuss best practices for writing agent code that is clean, modular, and reusable.

Clean Code Principles

- **Readability:**
  Write code that is easy to read and understand. Use clear variable names, consistent indentation, and meaningful comments.
- **Simplicity:**
  Keep functions and methods short and focused on a single task. Avoid unnecessary complexity.
- **Documentation:**
  Document your code with comments and docstrings. This not only helps others understand your code but also aids future you in maintaining it.

Modular Design

- **Separation of Concerns:**
  Divide your code into distinct modules where each module handles a

specific aspect of the agent's behavior. For example, separate communication, decision-making, and data processing into different functions or classes.

- **Loose Coupling:**
  Design modules so that they interact through well-defined interfaces. This makes it easier to update or replace parts of the system without affecting others.
- **Reusability:**
  Write functions and classes that can be reused across different agents or projects. Avoid hard-coding values and behaviors; instead, use parameters and configuration files.

Example: Modular Agent with Clean Code

Below is an example of an agent implemented with clean code principles and a modular design.

python

```python
# modular_agent.py

from langgraph import Agent

class ModularAgent(Agent):
    """
    An example of a modular and cleanly coded autonomous agent.
    """
    def __init__(self, name):
        super().__init__(name)
        self.task_count = 0

    def act(self):
        """
        Execute the agent's main action.
        """
        self._perform_task()
        self._log_action("Task performed")

    def _perform_task(self):
        """
        Private method to perform a task.
        """
```

```python
        self.task_count += 1
        print(f"{self.name} is performing task #{self.task_count}")

    def _log_action(self, message):
        """
        Private method to log an action.
        """
        # In a real-world scenario, this might write to a file or logging service
        print(f"[{self.name} LOG]: {message}")

    def receive_message(self, message, sender):
        """
        Handle incoming messages in a modular way.
        """
        self._process_message(message, sender)
        self._log_action("Message received")

    def _process_message(self, message, sender):
        """
        Private method to process an incoming message.
        """
        print(f"{self.name} received message from {sender.name}: {message}")

# Example usage:
if __name__ == "__main__":
    # Create an instance of ModularAgent
    agent = ModularAgent("Modular Agent")
    # Simulate performing an action
    agent.act()
    # Simulate receiving a message
    agent.receive_message("Hello, Modular Agent!", agent)
```

Explanation:

- **Modular Methods:**
  The ModularAgent class divides functionality into private helper methods (_perform_task, _log_action, and _process_message) that encapsulate specific behaviors.
- **Encapsulation:**
  By separating concerns, the code is easier to read, test, and maintain. Each method performs a single, well-defined function.

- **Logging and Messaging:**
  The agent logs its actions consistently, making it easier to trace behavior during testing and debugging.

Summary Table: Best Practices for Agent Coding

Best Practice	Description	Benefit
Clean Code	Write readable, simple, and well-documented code.	Enhances maintainability and reduces errors.
Modular Design	Divide code into independent, reusable modules with clear interfaces.	Facilitates updates, testing, and reusability.
Loose Coupling	Ensure modules interact via well-defined interfaces.	Minimizes interdependencies and simplifies changes.
Consistent Logging	Implement logging for key actions and events.	Aids in debugging and performance monitoring.

In this chapter, we examined the process of implementing autonomous agents in LangGraph through a comprehensive lifecycle: design, development, testing, and deployment. We illustrated the importance of each phase with detailed explanations, code examples, and a structured table to guide your efforts. Additionally, we discussed coding best practices that emphasize clean code, modular design, and reusability to ensure your agent implementations are efficient, maintainable, and scalable.

By following these guidelines and methodologies, you will be well-prepared to build robust, autonomous agents that can effectively operate within complex multi-agent systems powered by LangGraph.

7.3 Hands-On Code Walkthroughs and Examples

In this section, we provide practical, step-by-step code examples that illustrate how to build and coordinate autonomous agents using LangGraph. We start with a simple agent example and then move on to advanced scenarios involving agent interactions and multi-agent coordination.

Building a Simple Autonomous Agent

Let's begin by creating a basic autonomous agent that demonstrates essential functionalities such as performing tasks and handling messages. This simple agent will help you understand the structure and behavior expected by the LangGraph framework.

Example: A Basic Autonomous Agent

python

```python
# simple_agent.py

from langgraph import Agent

class SimpleAgent(Agent):
    """
    A basic autonomous agent that performs tasks and handles messages.
    """
    def __init__(self, name):
        # Initialize the base Agent with a given name
        super().__init__(name)
        self.task_counter = 0

    def act(self):
        """
        Perform a primary action, simulating task execution.
        """
        self.task_counter += 1
        print(f"{self.name} is executing task #{self.task_counter}")

    def receive_message(self, message, sender):
        """
        Handle an incoming message from another agent.
        """
        print(f"{self.name} received message from {sender.name}: {message}")

# Example usage:
if __name__ == "__main__":
    # Instantiate a simple agent
    agent = SimpleAgent("Agent One")
```

```python
# Simulate the agent performing an action
agent.act()
# Simulate receiving a message from itself for demonstration purposes
agent.receive_message("Hello, self!", agent)
```

Explanation:

- **Initialization:**
  The SimpleAgent class extends the LangGraph Agent class. The __init__ method initializes the agent with a name and sets up a counter to track the number of tasks completed.
- **Action Method (act):**
  The act() method simulates the execution of a task by incrementing the counter and printing a message. This is where you could integrate more complex behavior in a real-world scenario.
- **Message Handling (receive_message):**
  The receive_message() method processes incoming messages by printing the message and the sender's name.

Advanced Interaction Scenarios and Multi-Agent Coordination

For more complex systems, agents need to coordinate and interact with each other to perform tasks collectively. In this example, we create multiple agents that communicate and coordinate through a central mediator (simulated within the example code). This scenario demonstrates message passing and collaborative behavior.

Example: Multi-Agent Coordination with a Central Coordinator

python

```python
# coordinated_agents.py

from langgraph import Agent, GraphSystem

class CoordinatedAgent(Agent):
    """
    An agent that can communicate with other agents to coordinate tasks.
    """

    def __init__(self, name):
```

```python
        super().__init__(name)
        self.task_status = "idle"

    def act(self):
        """
        Perform a task and notify the system.
        """
        self.task_status = "active"
        print(f"{self.name} is performing its task.")
        # Simulate sending a message to the coordinator after completing a task
        self.send_message(f"{self.name} completed its task.",
target=self.system.coordinator)

    def receive_message(self, message, sender):
        """
        Process a message from another agent.
        """
        print(f"{self.name} received message from {sender.name}:
{message}")
        # Update internal state or respond based on the message
        if "override" in message:
            self.task_status = "overridden"
            print(f"{self.name} is adjusting its task based on coordinator
instruction.")

class CoordinatorAgent(Agent):
    """
    A central coordinator agent that manages multi-agent interactions.
    """

    def __init__(self, name):
        super().__init__(name)

    def receive_message(self, message, sender):
        """
        Receive messages from agents and make coordination decisions.
        """
        print(f"{self.name} received message from {sender.name}:
{message}")
        # For demonstration, the coordinator sends an override command back
to the sender
        if "completed" in message:
```

```python
        self.send_message("Override: Please adjust your task parameters.",
target=sender)

# Setting up the multi-agent system
if __name__ == "__main__":
    # Create the LangGraph system
    system = GraphSystem()

    # Instantiate a coordinator agent and assign it to the system
    coordinator = CoordinatorAgent("Coordinator")
    system.register_coordinator(coordinator)

    # Instantiate multiple coordinated agents and register them with the
system
    agent1 = CoordinatedAgent("Agent Alpha")
    agent2 = CoordinatedAgent("Agent Beta")

    system.add_agent(agent1)
    system.add_agent(agent2)

    # Link agents to the system (assume each agent gets a reference to the
system)
    agent1.system = system
    agent2.system = system
    coordinator.system = system

    # Simulate agents performing tasks
    agent1.act()
    agent2.act()
```

Explanation:

- **CoordinatedAgent:**
  Inherits from Agent and implements the act() method to perform a
  task. After completing its task, it sends a message to the coordinator
  agent.
- **CoordinatorAgent:**
  Also inherits from Agent and is designed to act as a central mediator.
  It processes messages from coordinated agents and, for this example,
  sends back an override command.
- **System Setup:**
  A GraphSystem instance is created, and the coordinator agent is

registered as the central coordinator. Multiple coordinated agents are added to the system, and each agent is linked to the system for communication.

- **Interaction Flow:**
  When a coordinated agent completes its task, it sends a message to the coordinator, which then replies with a command, demonstrating multi-agent coordination.

7.4 Integrating External APIs and Data Sources

Modern autonomous systems often need to interact with external data sources, such as databases, IoT devices, and third-party services. This integration expands the capabilities of your agents, enabling them to make data-driven decisions, access real-time information, and interact with other systems.

Connecting to Databases

Example: Integrating a SQL Database with an Agent

In this example, we demonstrate how an agent can query a SQL database using Python's sqlite3 module to retrieve data that may influence its behavior.

python

```python
# database_agent.py

import sqlite3
from langgraph import Agent

class DatabaseAgent(Agent):
    """
    An agent that connects to a SQL database to fetch data.
    """
    def __init__(self, name, db_path):
        super().__init__(name)
        self.db_path = db_path

    def fetch_data(self, query):
```

```
"""
    Connect to the database, execute a query, and return the results.
    """
    try:
        # Connect to the SQLite database
        connection = sqlite3.connect(self.db_path)
        cursor = connection.cursor()
        # Execute the provided query
        cursor.execute(query)
        results = cursor.fetchall()
        connection.close()
        print(f"{self.name} fetched data: {results}")
        return results
    except sqlite3.Error as e:
        print(f"Database error: {e}")
        return None

# Example usage:
if __name__ == "__main__":
    # Assuming you have a SQLite database file 'data.db'
    db_agent = DatabaseAgent("DB Agent", "data.db")
    # Example query to retrieve all records from a table named 'sensors'
    db_agent.fetch_data("SELECT * FROM sensors;")
```

Explanation:

- **Database Connection:**
  The DatabaseAgent class connects to a SQLite database using the file path provided during initialization.
- **Data Retrieval:**
  The fetch_data() method executes a SQL query and fetches results. Error handling ensures that any issues with the database are caught and reported.
- **Usage Scenario:**
  An agent can use this data to adjust its behavior based on sensor readings or historical data.

Connecting to IoT Devices

Example: Integrating with an IoT Device via HTTP API

In many applications, agents need to interact with IoT devices. This example uses Python's requests library to simulate an agent querying data from an IoT device's REST API.

python

```python
# iot_agent.py

import requests
from langgraph import Agent

class IoTAgent(Agent):
    """
    An agent that retrieves data from an IoT device via its REST API.
    """
    def __init__(self, name, device_api_url):
        super().__init__(name)
        self.device_api_url = device_api_url

    def get_sensor_data(self):
        """
        Send an HTTP GET request to the IoT device and return the sensor data.
        """
        try:
            response = requests.get(self.device_api_url)
            if response.status_code == 200:
                data = response.json()
                print(f"{self.name} received sensor data: {data}")
                return data
            else:
                print(f"{self.name} error: Received status code {response.status_code}")
                return None
        except requests.RequestException as e:
            print(f"{self.name} encountered an error: {e}")
            return None

# Example usage:
if __name__ == "__main__":
    # Replace with the actual API endpoint of your IoT device
    api_url = "http://iot-device.local/api/sensor"
```

```python
iot_agent = IoTAgent("IoT Agent", api_url)
iot_agent.get_sensor_data()
```

Explanation:

- **HTTP API Integration:**
  The IoTAgent class uses the requests library to perform an HTTP GET request to an IoT device's API endpoint.
- **Data Processing:**
  On receiving a successful response (HTTP 200), the agent parses the JSON data and prints it. Error handling ensures network issues or non-200 responses are properly managed.
- **Practical Use:**
  Agents can leverage this method to obtain real-time sensor data, which can then influence decision-making processes.

Connecting to Third-Party Services

Example: Integrating with a Weather API

Third-party services such as weather APIs can provide valuable context for agent decisions. In this example, an agent queries a weather API to obtain current weather conditions, which could be used to adjust behaviors in a smart environment.

python

```python
# weather_agent.py

import requests
from langgraph import Agent

class WeatherAgent(Agent):
    """
    An agent that fetches current weather data from a third-party API.
    """

    def __init__(self, name, api_key, location):
        super().__init__(name)
        self.api_key = api_key
        self.location = location
```

```python
        self.base_url = "http://api.openweathermap.org/data/2.5/weather"

    def get_weather(self):
        """
        Fetch the current weather data for the specified location.
        """
        params = {
            'q': self.location,
            'appid': self.api_key,
            'units': 'metric'
        }
        try:
            response = requests.get(self.base_url, params=params)
            if response.status_code == 200:
                weather_data = response.json()
                print(f"{self.name} weather data: {weather_data}")
                return weather_data
            else:
                print(f"{self.name} error: Status code {response.status_code}")
                return None
        except requests.RequestException as e:
            print(f"{self.name} encountered an error: {e}")
            return None

# Example usage:
if __name__ == "__main__":
    # Replace with your actual API key and desired location
    api_key = "your_openweathermap_api_key"
    location = "London"
    weather_agent = WeatherAgent("Weather Agent", api_key, location)
    weather_agent.get_weather()
```

Explanation:

- **Third-Party API Integration:**
  The WeatherAgent class integrates with OpenWeatherMap's API by sending an HTTP GET request with necessary parameters such as location and API key.
- **Data Retrieval:**
  Upon receiving a valid response, the agent processes the JSON data to extract weather information.

- **Usage Considerations:**
  This example demonstrates how agents can use external data to adapt behaviors (e.g., adjusting building controls based on temperature or precipitation).

Summary Table: Integrating External APIs and Data Sources

Integration Type	Example Library/Tool	Description	Typical Use Cases
SQL Database	sqlite3	Connects to a local or remote SQL database to fetch or store data.	Storing sensor logs, historical performance data.
IoT Devices	requests	Accesses IoT devices through REST APIs to retrieve real-time data.	Monitoring sensor data, controlling smart devices.
Third-Party Services	requests	Integrates with external services (e.g., weather APIs) to get contextual information.	Adjusting system behavior based on external factors.

In this section, we provided comprehensive hands-on code walkthroughs and examples for implementing autonomous agents with LangGraph. We demonstrated how to build a simple agent and then expanded into advanced interaction scenarios that enable multi-agent coordination. Additionally, we explored methods for integrating external APIs and data sources, including databases, IoT devices, and third-party services, to enrich agent functionality with real-time and contextual data.

These practical examples, along with clear code explanations and summary tables, aim to equip you with the knowledge needed to build, extend, and integrate sophisticated autonomous agents within your LangGraph-based systems. This approach ensures your multi-agent system is not only robust and capable of internal coordination but also well-connected with the external environment to drive intelligent, data-informed decisions.

Chapter 8: Advanced LangGraph Techniques and Patterns

In this chapter, we explore advanced techniques for extending and optimizing LangGraph-based systems. We first examine how to customize graph models to accommodate complex, dynamic scenarios where agents and relationships evolve over time. Then, we delve into implementing event-driven architectures, a critical approach for managing asynchronous workflows, events, and subscriptions in large-scale autonomous systems.

8.1 Customizing Graph Models for Complex Scenarios

As multi-agent systems evolve, the underlying graph models must be flexible enough to handle dynamic changes and evolving structures. This section discusses strategies for adapting graph models in LangGraph to meet complex and changing requirements.

Handling Dynamic Changes and Evolving Structures

Real-world systems are rarely static; new agents can be added, existing ones may fail or be removed, and the relationships between agents can change over time. To manage these dynamics, consider the following strategies:

1. **Dynamic Node and Edge Management:**
   - **Addition and Removal:**
     Your graph model should support the real-time addition or removal of nodes (agents) and edges (relationships). This is essential for adapting to changes such as scaling up (adding agents) or handling failures (removing agents).
   - **Attribute Updates:**
     Agents often have properties that change over time, such as status, load, or location. The graph should allow for efficient updates of node attributes.
2. **Evolving Relationship Structures:**
   - **Temporal Edges:**
     In some scenarios, relationships have a time component—such as a connection that is only valid for a certain period.

Storing timestamps or validity durations with edges can help manage such transient relationships.

- ○ **Weighted Relationships:**
  As interactions evolve, the strength or importance of a relationship might change. Adjusting the weights of edges dynamically can reflect shifts in communication frequency or dependency strength.

3. **Partitioning and Hierarchical Graphs:**
   - ○ **Clustering:**
     For large systems, grouping agents into clusters or communities can improve performance and clarity. Hierarchical graphs allow you to view the system at different levels of granularity.
   - ○ **Subgraphs:**
     In complex environments, it can be beneficial to isolate parts of the graph for independent processing or analysis. Subgraphs can represent different operational zones or functional modules.

Example: Dynamic Graph Updates with NetworkX

Below is a code example that demonstrates how to create a dynamic graph model using Python's NetworkX library. This example simulates adding and removing agents, updating attributes, and managing evolving relationships.

python

```python
import networkx as nx
import matplotlib.pyplot as plt

# Initialize a dynamic graph
dynamic_graph = nx.Graph()

# Function to add an agent (node) with initial attributes
def add_agent(agent_id, status="active", zone="default"):
    dynamic_graph.add_node(agent_id, status=status, zone=zone)
    print(f"Added {agent_id} with status: {status} and zone: {zone}")

# Function to remove an agent (node)
def remove_agent(agent_id):
    if dynamic_graph.has_node(agent_id):
        dynamic_graph.remove_node(agent_id)
```

```python
        print(f"Removed {agent_id}")
    else:
        print(f"Agent {agent_id} does not exist.")

# Function to update an agent's attribute
def update_agent_status(agent_id, new_status):
    if dynamic_graph.has_node(agent_id):
        dynamic_graph.nodes[agent_id]['status'] = new_status
        print(f"Updated {agent_id} status to {new_status}")
    else:
        print(f"Agent {agent_id} does not exist.")

# Function to add or update an edge with a weight and timestamp attribute
def add_or_update_relationship(source, target, weight=1.0,
timestamp="2025-02-08T00:00:00Z"):
    dynamic_graph.add_edge(source, target, weight=weight,
timestamp=timestamp)
    print(f"Added/Updated relationship: {source} -> {target} with weight
{weight} at {timestamp}")

# Add initial agents
add_agent("Agent_1", status="active", zone="A")
add_agent("Agent_2", status="active", zone="A")
add_agent("Agent_3", status="idle", zone="B")

# Add relationships between agents
add_or_update_relationship("Agent_1", "Agent_2", weight=0.8,
timestamp="2025-02-08T12:00:00Z")
add_or_update_relationship("Agent_2", "Agent_3", weight=0.5,
timestamp="2025-02-08T12:05:00Z")

# Update an agent's status dynamically
update_agent_status("Agent_3", "active")

# Remove an agent
remove_agent("Agent_2")

# Visualize the dynamic graph
plt.figure(figsize=(8, 6))
pos = nx.spring_layout(dynamic_graph)
nx.draw(dynamic_graph, pos, with_labels=True, node_color='lightgreen',
edge_color='gray', node_size=2000, font_size=10)
```

```
# Draw edge labels to show relationship weights and timestamps
edge_labels = { (u, v): f"{data['weight']} @ {data['timestamp']}" for u, v,
data in dynamic_graph.edges(data=True) }
nx.draw_networkx_edge_labels(dynamic_graph, pos,
edge_labels=edge_labels, font_color='blue')

plt.title("Dynamic Multi-Agent Graph Model")
plt.show()
```

Explanation:

- **Dynamic Operations:**
  The functions add_agent(), remove_agent(), and
  update_agent_status() manage node operations. The
  add_or_update_relationship() function handles edge creation and
  updates, including custom attributes such as weight and timestamp.
- **Visualization:**
  The graph is visualized using a spring layout, and edge labels display
  the weight and timestamp, illustrating how relationships can evolve
  over time.

8.2 Implementing Event-Driven Architectures

Event-driven architectures are vital for building responsive and scalable
multi-agent systems. In such systems, agents react to events—changes or
occurrences within the environment—by subscribing to and processing these
events asynchronously.

Managing Events and Subscriptions

An event-driven architecture typically involves the following components:

- **Event Publishers:**
  Agents or external systems that generate events. These events can
  range from sensor readings to task completions.
- **Event Subscribers:**
  Agents that register interest in specific types of events and execute
  corresponding actions when these events occur.

- **Event Dispatcher:**
  A central component that manages event subscriptions and delivers events to the appropriate subscribers.

Asynchronous Workflows

Handling events asynchronously allows agents to remain responsive and efficient, especially in distributed environments where operations may take varying amounts of time. Asynchronous workflows can be implemented using Python's asyncio library, enabling non-blocking operations and concurrent event processing.

Example: Event-Driven System Using an Asynchronous Dispatcher

Below is a code example demonstrating an event-driven architecture with asynchronous event handling. This example simulates event subscription, publication, and asynchronous processing using asyncio.

python

```python
import asyncio

class AsyncEventDispatcher:
    """
    A simple asynchronous event dispatcher that manages event subscriptions
    and publication.
    """
    def __init__(self):
        self.subscribers = {}

    def subscribe(self, event_type, handler):
        """
        Subscribe a handler to a specific event type.
        """
        if event_type not in self.subscribers:
            self.subscribers[event_type] = []
        self.subscribers[event_type].append(handler)
        print(f"Subscribed handler for event: {event_type}")

    async def publish(self, event_type, data):
        """
        Publish an event to all subscribers asynchronously.
```

```python
    """
    if event_type in self.subscribers:
        await asyncio.gather(*(handler(data) for handler in
self.subscribers[event_type]))
    else:
        print(f"No subscribers for event: {event_type}")

# Define sample asynchronous event handlers
async def temperature_handler(data):
    await asyncio.sleep(1)  # Simulate processing delay
    print(f"Temperature handler processed data: {data}")

async def humidity_handler(data):
    await asyncio.sleep(1)  # Simulate processing delay
    print(f"Humidity handler processed data: {data}")

# Example usage of the asynchronous event dispatcher
async def main():
    dispatcher = AsyncEventDispatcher()
    # Subscribe handlers to specific events
    dispatcher.subscribe("temperature_change", temperature_handler)
    dispatcher.subscribe("humidity_change", humidity_handler)

    # Publish events concurrently
    await dispatcher.publish("temperature_change", {"temp": 22})
    await dispatcher.publish("humidity_change", {"humidity": 55})

# Run the asynchronous main function
if __name__ == "__main__":
    asyncio.run(main())
```

Explanation:

- **AsyncEventDispatcher:**
  This class manages subscriptions and event publication. The
  subscribe() method registers event handlers, and the publish() method
  asynchronously calls all subscribed handlers using asyncio.gather().
- **Asynchronous Handlers:**
  The temperature_handler() and humidity_handler() functions
  simulate event processing with a delay using await asyncio.sleep(1).
  This mimics real-world scenarios where processing time may vary.

- **Asynchronous Workflow:**
  The main() function demonstrates subscribing to events and publishing them asynchronously. The use of asyncio.run() ensures that the event loop is managed correctly.

Benefits of an Event-Driven Architecture

Aspect	Benefit
Responsiveness	Asynchronous handling allows agents to process events without blocking other operations.
Scalability	The decoupled nature of event-driven systems supports a large number of agents and events concurrently.
Flexibility	Agents can subscribe to and filter events based on interest, making the system adaptable to dynamic changes.
Loose Coupling	Publishers and subscribers operate independently, promoting modularity and ease of maintenance.

In this chapter, we explored advanced techniques for customizing graph models and implementing event-driven architectures within LangGraph. We discussed how to manage dynamic changes and evolving structures by updating nodes, edges, and their attributes in real time. A detailed code example illustrated the process of building a dynamic graph model with NetworkX.

Next, we examined the fundamentals of event-driven architectures—focusing on managing events, subscriptions, and asynchronous workflows. By leveraging Python's asyncio library, we demonstrated how to build an asynchronous event dispatcher that enables responsive, non-blocking event handling.

Together, these advanced techniques and patterns empower you to design and implement sophisticated multi-agent systems that are adaptable, scalable, and capable of responding to real-time changes and events in complex environments.

8.3 Complex Decision-Making and AI Integration

As multi-agent systems become increasingly sophisticated, simple rule-based decision-making often proves insufficient for handling complex scenarios.

Integrating advanced techniques such as machine learning (ML) and predictive analytics can empower your agents to make more nuanced and proactive decisions. In this section, we explore strategies to incorporate AI techniques into LangGraph and enhance agent decision-making.

Incorporating Machine Learning

Overview

Machine learning models enable agents to learn from historical data and predict future events or behaviors. By integrating ML into your agents, you can:

- **Improve Adaptability:**
  Agents learn from past interactions and optimize future decisions
- **Enhance Predictive Capabilities:**
  Predict outcomes like system load, sensor failures, or environmental changes.
- **Automate Complex Tasks:**
  Automatically classify events, optimize routes, or detect anomalies.

Integration Strategies

1. **Pre-trained Models:**
   Use pre-trained models for tasks such as image recognition, anomaly detection, or forecasting. These models can be integrated via libraries such as TensorFlow, PyTorch, or scikit-learn.
2. **Online Learning:**
   Implement models that update continuously as new data becomes available. This approach is especially useful in dynamic environments where conditions change rapidly.
3. **Hybrid Decision-Making:**
   Combine rule-based logic with machine learning predictions. For example, an agent might use rules to manage routine tasks and rely on ML models for edge cases or uncertainty.

Example: Integrating a Predictive Analytics Model

Below is an example of a LangGraph agent that incorporates a simple machine learning model using scikit-learn. In this scenario, the agent uses a pre-trained linear regression model to predict the future value of a sensor reading, allowing it to adjust its behavior proactively.

python

```python
# ml_agent.py

import numpy as np
from langgraph import Agent
from sklearn.linear_model import LinearRegression
import pickle

class MLAgent(Agent):
    """
    An agent that integrates a machine learning model to predict sensor readings.
    """
    def __init__(self, name, model_path):
        super().__init__(name)
        # Load a pre-trained model from a pickle file
        with open(model_path, 'rb') as file:
            self.model = pickle.load(file)
        # Initialize historical sensor data (for simulation purposes)
        self.sensor_history = []

    def update_sensor_data(self, new_value):
        """
        Update the agent's sensor data history and predict the next sensor reading.
        """
        self.sensor_history.append(new_value)
        print(f"{self.name} received new sensor data: {new_value}")
        # Only predict if we have enough data points
        if len(self.sensor_history) >= 5:
            self.predict_next_value()

    def predict_next_value(self):
        """
        Use the ML model to predict the next sensor value.
        """
        # Prepare the input features (e.g., using the last 5 readings)
        input_data = np.array(self.sensor_history[-5:]).reshape(1, -1)
```

```python
        predicted_value = self.model.predict(input_data)[0]
        print(f"{self.name} predicts the next sensor value will be:
{predicted_value:.2f}")
        # Based on the prediction, take appropriate action (this is a placeholder)
        if predicted_value > 50:
            self.take_preventive_action()
        else:
            print(f"{self.name} continues normal operations.")

    def take_preventive_action(self):
        """
        Execute a preventive action based on the prediction.
        """
        print(f"{self.name} is taking preventive action due to high predicted
sensor value.")

# Example usage:
if __name__ == "__main__":
    # Assume a pre-trained linear regression model is saved as 'model.pkl'
    ml_agent = MLAgent("ML Agent", "model.pkl")

    # Simulate incoming sensor data
    sensor_values = [45, 47, 49, 50, 52, 55]
    for value in sensor_values:
        ml_agent.update_sensor_data(value)
```

Explanation:

- **Model Loading:**
  The MLAgent loads a pre-trained linear regression model from a file
  using Python's pickle module.
- **Sensor Data Update:**
  The update_sensor_data() method appends new sensor readings to a
  history list. Once there are enough data points, it calls
  predict_next_value().
- **Prediction and Action:**
  The agent uses the last five sensor values to predict the next value. If
  the prediction exceeds a threshold, it takes preventive action.
- **Hybrid Decision-Making:**
  The agent combines data-driven predictions with rule-based actions,
  demonstrating a hybrid approach to decision-making.

8.4 Debugging, Monitoring, and Real-Time Analytics

Effective debugging and monitoring are crucial for maintaining the reliability and performance of a multi-agent system. Real-time analytics provide insights into system behavior, enabling proactive maintenance and rapid problem resolution.

Tools and Techniques for Live System Analysis

1. **Logging and Auditing:**
   o **Centralized Logging:**
     Aggregate logs from all agents into a central system using tools like ELK Stack (Elasticsearch, Logstash, Kibana) or Splunk.
   o **Structured Logging:**
     Use structured formats (e.g., JSON) for logs to facilitate easy parsing and analysis.
2. **Monitoring Systems:**
   o **Real-Time Dashboards:**
     Implement dashboards using tools like Grafana or Kibana to visualize metrics such as response times, error rates, and system load.
   o **Alerts and Notifications:**
     Set up alerts to notify administrators when critical thresholds are exceeded, using systems like Prometheus Alertmanager.
3. **Tracing and Profiling:**
   o **Distributed Tracing:**
     Use tools like Jaeger or Zipkin to trace requests and interactions across agents, helping to identify bottlenecks and latency issues.
   o **Performance Profiling:**
     Employ profiling tools (e.g., cProfile for Python) to monitor resource usage and optimize code performance.
4. **Debugging Techniques:**
   o **Live Debugging:**
     Use interactive debugging tools (e.g., pdb for Python) to inspect the state of agents during execution.
   o **Simulated Environments:**
     Create test harnesses and simulation environments to replicate

production issues and test fixes without impacting live systems.

Example: Integrating Logging and Real-Time Monitoring

Below is an example demonstrating how to integrate basic logging and real-time monitoring into a LangGraph agent. This example uses Python's built-in logging module and simulates real-time metric updates.

python

```python
# monitoring_agent.py

import logging
import time
from langgraph import Agent

# Configure logging
logging.basicConfig(level=logging.INFO, format='%(asctime)s - %(name)s - %(levelname)s - %(message)s')
logger = logging.getLogger("MonitoringAgent")

class MonitoringAgent(Agent):
    """
    An agent that performs tasks and logs detailed metrics for real-time monitoring.
    """
    def __init__(self, name):
        super().__init__(name)
        self.task_counter = 0
        self.start_time = time.time()

    def act(self):
        """
        Perform a task and log execution metrics.
        """
        self.task_counter += 1
        current_time = time.time()
        elapsed_time = current_time - self.start_time
        logger.info(f"{self.name} executed task #{self.task_counter} in {elapsed_time:.2f} seconds")
        # Simulate performing a task
```

```python
        time.sleep(0.5)  # Simulating task duration

    def receive_message(self, message, sender):
        """
        Handle incoming messages and log the interaction.
        """
        logger.info(f"{self.name} received message from {sender.name}:
{message}")

# Example usage:
if __name__ == "__main__":
    monitoring_agent = MonitoringAgent("Monitoring Agent")

    # Simulate a series of actions and message exchanges
    for _ in range(3):
        monitoring_agent.act()

    # Simulate receiving a message
    monitoring_agent.receive_message("System check complete.",
monitoring_agent)
```

Explanation:

- **Logging Setup:**
  The logging configuration is set up to include timestamps, agent names, and log levels. This makes it easier to analyze logs in real time.
- **Metric Logging:**
  The act() method logs the task number and the elapsed time since the agent started. This can help monitor performance and identify delays.
- **Real-Time Insights:**
  By logging each action and message receipt, administrators can use tools like Grafana (integrated with a logging backend) to create real-time dashboards for monitoring system health.

Summary Table: Debugging, Monitoring, and Real-Time Analytics Tools

Category	Tool/Technique	Description	Benefits
Logging	Python logging, ELK Stack, Splunk	Collect and aggregate structured logs for analysis.	Facilitates debugging, auditing, and historical analysis.
Monitoring	Grafana, Kibana, Prometheus	Visualize system metrics and set up alerts for critical events.	Real-time insights into system performance and reliability.
Tracing	Jaeger, Zipkin	Trace requests across distributed agents to identify bottlenecks.	Helps in diagnosing latency and inter-service communication issues.
Profiling	cProfile, Py-Spy	Monitor CPU and memory usage to optimize performance.	Identifies resource-intensive parts of the code.
Debugging	pdb, VSCode Debugger	Step through code execution interactively to find and fix issues.	Accelerates troubleshooting and reduces downtime.

Integrating advanced AI techniques and robust monitoring practices elevates your LangGraph-based multi-agent systems to handle complex, dynamic environments effectively. In this section, we discussed how incorporating machine learning and predictive analytics enables agents to make informed, proactive decisions. We demonstrated this through an example that uses a pre-trained model to predict sensor readings and adjust behavior accordingly.

Additionally, we explored tools and techniques for real-time debugging, monitoring, and analytics. By integrating logging, real-time dashboards, and distributed tracing into your system, you can maintain high levels of performance and reliability while rapidly addressing issues as they arise.

Together, these advanced strategies empower your multi-agent system to not only respond to current conditions but also predict and adapt to future challenges, ensuring optimal operation in complex real-world scenarios.

Chapter 9: Principles of Scalability in Multi-Agent Systems

Scaling a multi-agent system effectively is critical for ensuring that it can handle increased workloads, maintain performance, and deliver high availability even in the face of failures. In this chapter, we will explore the fundamental challenges to scalability in distributed systems, followed by best practices and architectural patterns to design scalable and highly available systems.

9.1 Understanding Scalability Challenges

When scaling multi-agent systems, it is essential to understand the common bottlenecks and challenges that distributed environments face. These challenges can limit performance and reduce the reliability of the system if not addressed properly.

Bottlenecks in Distributed Systems

Distributed systems, including multi-agent systems, often encounter several key bottlenecks:

1. **Network Latency and Bandwidth Constraints:**
   - **Latency:** Communication delays between agents across different network nodes can slow down system responsiveness.
   - **Bandwidth:** Limited network bandwidth may restrict the amount of data that can be exchanged between agents, leading to congestion.
2. **Centralized Coordination Bottlenecks:**
   - **Single Point of Failure:** In architectures where a central coordinator manages all interactions, the coordinator can become a bottleneck. If it fails or becomes overloaded, the entire system may suffer.
   - **Scalability Limits:** A centralized control mechanism may struggle to handle a large number of agents, resulting in delayed decision-making and reduced performance.
3. **Resource Contention:**

- o **CPU and Memory Limitations:** As more agents are added, the system may experience resource contention, where CPU and memory resources become strained, leading to slower processing times.
- o **I/O Bound Operations:** Heavy input/output operations, such as logging, data storage, or external API calls, can also become a limiting factor.

4. **Synchronization and Coordination Overhead:**
    - o **Concurrency Issues:** Ensuring that multiple agents work together without conflicts may require synchronization mechanisms that introduce overhead.
    - o **Consistency Requirements:** Maintaining data consistency across distributed nodes can lead to delays if complex consensus algorithms or distributed transactions are used.

Example: Identifying a Bottleneck

Consider a scenario where a central server is used to coordinate the actions of 1,000 agents. If each agent sends status updates every second, the central server may become overwhelmed by the sheer volume of messages, leading to increased latency and potential message loss. This scenario illustrates a typical centralized coordination bottleneck.

Summary Table: Common Scalability Bottlenecks

Bottleneck Type	Description	Impact on System
Network Latency	Delays in data transmission across nodes.	Slower response times; degraded system performance.
Bandwidth Limitations	Restricted data flow due to network constraints.	Communication bottlenecks; increased congestion.
Centralized Coordination	Overreliance on a single control node.	Single point of failure; scalability limits.
Resource Contention	Limited CPU, memory, or I/O capacity when many agents operate simultaneously.	Slower processing; potential system crashes.

Bottleneck Type	Description	Impact on System
Synchronization Overhead	Overhead from ensuring consistency and coordination among agents.	Increased delays; reduced throughput.

9.2 Designing for Scalability and High Availability

To overcome the challenges outlined above, multi-agent systems must be designed with scalability and high availability in mind. This involves selecting appropriate architectural patterns, implementing best practices, and utilizing effective tools to balance the load and ensure continuous operation.

Best Practices for Scalability

1. **Horizontal Scaling:**
   o **Description:**
      Distribute the workload by adding more nodes or agents to the system.
   o **Implementation:**
      Use techniques such as clustering or partitioning the agent population. For example, dividing agents into groups that operate independently can reduce the load on any single component.
2. **Load Balancing:**
   o **Description:**
      Distribute incoming tasks evenly across agents or nodes to prevent any single entity from becoming overloaded.
   o **Implementation:**
      Implement load balancers (hardware or software-based) to distribute requests in a round-robin or weighted manner.
3. **Modular Architecture:**
   o **Description:**
      Design the system as a collection of loosely coupled modules or microservices.
   o **Implementation:**
      Each module handles a specific function (e.g., communication, data processing) and can be scaled independently.
4. **Caching Strategies:**

- o **Description:**
  Store frequently accessed data in memory to reduce redundant processing and data retrieval operations.
- o **Implementation:**
  Use in-memory data stores like Redis or Memcached to cache results and reduce database load.

5. **Asynchronous Processing:**
   - o **Description:**
     Handle tasks asynchronously to prevent blocking and improve system responsiveness.
   - o **Implementation:**
     Utilize asynchronous programming models and frameworks (e.g., Python's asyncio) to manage concurrent operations efficiently.

Architectural Patterns for High Availability

1. **Decentralized Architectures:**
   - o **Description:**
     Distribute control and decision-making among agents to eliminate a single point of failure.
   - o **Benefits:**
     Increased resilience and scalability, as the system can continue operating even if one node fails.
2. **Hybrid Architectures:**
   - o **Description:**
     Combine centralized and decentralized elements. A central coordinator may manage high-level tasks, while agents operate autonomously for routine operations.
   - o **Benefits:**
     Balances the advantages of both approaches, ensuring overall control while enabling local responsiveness.
3. **Redundancy and Failover Mechanisms:**
   - o **Description:**
     Incorporate redundant components that can take over in the event of a failure.
   - o **Benefits:**
     Minimizes downtime and ensures continuous operation. Techniques such as active-active or active-passive failover configurations can be used.

Example: Simulating Horizontal Scaling with Round-Robin Load Balancing

Below is a Python code example that simulates distributing tasks among a set of agents using a round-robin approach.

python

```python
# load_balancer.py

from langgraph import Agent, GraphSystem

class LoadBalancingAgent(Agent):
    """
    An agent that simulates processing a task.
    """
    def __init__(self, name):
        super().__init__(name)

    def process_task(self, task):
        """
        Simulate processing a given task.
        """
        print(f"{self.name} is processing task: {task}")

# Create a simple load balancing function using round-robin scheduling
def round_robin_scheduler(agents, tasks):
    """
    Distribute tasks among agents using round-robin scheduling.

    Parameters:
    - agents: List of agent instances.
    - tasks: List of tasks to be processed.
    """
    num_agents = len(agents)
    for index, task in enumerate(tasks):
        # Determine the agent to process the current task
        agent = agents[index % num_agents]
        agent.process_task(task)

# Example usage:
if __name__ == "__main__":
```

```
# Create a LangGraph system (for context; in real scenarios, this would be
more complex)
system = GraphSystem()

# Instantiate a list of load balancing agents
agents = [LoadBalancingAgent(f"Agent_{i}") for i in range(1, 4)]
for agent in agents:
    system.add_agent(agent)

# Define a list of tasks to be processed
tasks = [f"Task_{i}" for i in range(1, 10)]

# Distribute tasks using round-robin scheduling
round_robin_scheduler(agents, tasks)
```

Explanation:

- **Agent Definition:**
  The LoadBalancingAgent class extends the LangGraph Agent class
  and defines a process_task() method to simulate task processing.
- **Round-Robin Scheduler:**
  The round_robin_scheduler() function takes a list of agents and a list
  of tasks. It distributes the tasks in a round-robin fashion by assigning
  each task to an agent based on the task index modulo the number of
  agents.
- **System Setup:**
  A simple GraphSystem instance is created for context. Agents are
  added to the system, and tasks are processed, simulating horizontal
  scaling through load balancing.

**Summary Table: Best Practices and Architectural Patterns for
Scalability**

Aspect	Best Practice / Pattern	Description	Benefits
Horizontal Scaling	Adding more agents/nodes	Distribute workload across multiple agents.	Improved performance and capacity.
Load Balancing	Round-robin, weighted distribution	Evenly distribute tasks among agents.	Prevents overload of any single agent.

Aspect	Best Practice / Pattern	Description	Benefits
Modular Architecture	Microservices, independent modules	Design system components to operate independently.	Easier scaling and maintenance.
Decentralized Architecture	Distributed control	Eliminate central points of failure by distributing decision-making.	Increased resilience and fault tolerance.
Redundancy & Failover	Active-active, active-passive setups	Implement redundant components to take over during failures.	Minimizes downtime; enhances system reliability.
Asynchronous Processing	Non-blocking I/O, async frameworks	Use asynchronous methods to process tasks concurrently.	Improves responsiveness and overall throughput.

Designing scalable and highly available multi-agent systems involves understanding the inherent challenges of distributed environments and adopting best practices and architectural patterns to overcome them. In this chapter, we explored common scalability bottlenecks such as network latency, centralized coordination challenges, resource contention, and synchronization overhead.

We then discussed strategies for designing systems that are scalable and resilient, including horizontal scaling, load balancing, modular and decentralized architectures, and redundancy with failover mechanisms. A practical code example demonstrated a round-robin load balancing approach to distribute tasks among agents, showcasing how these principles can be implemented in a LangGraph-based system.

By applying these principles and best practices, you can ensure that your multi-agent systems not only meet current performance requirements but are also prepared to scale and remain available as demands increase and environmental conditions evolve.

9.3 Case Studies in Scalable LangGraph Deployments

Real-world deployments of multi-agent systems using LangGraph offer valuable insights into both the challenges and effective strategies for scaling distributed architectures. In this section, we review several case studies that highlight practical implementations of LangGraph in scalable environments. These case studies not only showcase the successful application of LangGraph in diverse domains but also provide lessons learned that can guide future deployments.

Case Study 1: Smart City Traffic Management System

Overview

A metropolitan city implemented a traffic management system using LangGraph to coordinate thousands of autonomous agents, each representing traffic signals, cameras, and environmental sensors. The goal was to optimize traffic flow, reduce congestion, and improve emergency response times.

Deployment Details

- **System Scale:**
  Over 5,000 autonomous agents deployed across the city.
- **Architecture:**
  A hybrid architecture was used where a central control unit managed high-level policies (e.g., adjusting signal timings citywide), while local clusters of agents (representing intersections) operated autonomously for real-time adjustments.
- **Key Technologies:**
  - **LangGraph Framework:** Managed agent creation, communication, and coordination.
  - **Distributed Data Stores:** For real-time sensor data and historical traffic patterns.
  - **Asynchronous Communication:** Leveraged to handle high volumes of real-time messages with minimal latency.

Challenges Encountered

- **Network Latency and Bandwidth:**
  With agents distributed over a large geographical area, ensuring timely communication was a major challenge.
- **Central Bottlenecks:**
  The central coordinator risked becoming a single point of failure under peak loads.
- **Data Overload:**
  Handling and processing the massive influx of sensor data required robust data management strategies.

Solutions and Lessons Learned

- **Decentralized Clustering:**
  By partitioning the network into local clusters, each managed by a regional coordinator, the system reduced latency and improved fault tolerance.
- **Load Balancing:**
  Implementing round-robin and weighted load balancing across communication channels prevented any single node from becoming overloaded.
- **Real-Time Analytics:**
  Integration with real-time analytics platforms allowed for immediate adjustments to traffic signals based on current conditions.

Key Takeaways

- **Distributed architectures are essential** for managing large-scale deployments.
- **Local autonomy within clusters** minimizes the risk of central bottlenecks.
- **Robust data and communication management** is critical to handle high volumes of real-time information.

Case Study 2: Industrial IoT in Manufacturing

Overview

A large manufacturing plant deployed a multi-agent system to monitor and control various stages of the production line. LangGraph was used to coordinate sensors, robotic arms, and quality control systems to ensure operational efficiency and product quality.

Deployment Details

- **System Scale:**
  Hundreds of agents managing different production units and machinery.
- **Architecture:**
  A modular and decentralized architecture was chosen to allow each production unit to operate independently while still sharing critical data with a central monitoring system.
- **Key Technologies:**
  - **LangGraph Framework:** Enabled dynamic agent management and inter-agent communication.
  - **In-Memory Data Caching:** Reduced latency in accessing frequently used production data.
  - **Asynchronous Event Handling:** Managed irregular production events and equipment failures.

Challenges Encountered

- **Resource Contention:**
  High processing demands from simultaneous operations led to CPU and memory constraints.
- **Synchronization Overhead:**
  Coordinating actions across machines with differing operational speeds proved challenging.
- **System Downtime:**
  Any delay or failure in one production unit could potentially affect the overall manufacturing process.

Solutions and Lessons Learned

- **Modular Design:**
  Each production unit was designed as an independent module, reducing interdependencies and allowing for targeted scalability.
- **Asynchronous Processing:**
  Implementing asynchronous workflows allowed the system to handle tasks concurrently, thereby reducing delays.

- **Redundancy and Failover:**
  Critical production units were equipped with backup systems that could take over in the event of a failure, ensuring high availability.

Key Takeaways

- **Modularity and decentralization** improve resilience and allow for focused scalability.
- **Asynchronous processing** is essential in environments with unpredictable loads.
- **Redundancy and failover mechanisms** are critical to maintain continuous operation in industrial settings.

Case Study 3: Distributed Financial Trading System

Overview

A financial services firm implemented a distributed algorithmic trading system using LangGraph to manage high-frequency trading operations. Autonomous agents were responsible for executing trades, monitoring market conditions, and adjusting strategies in real time.

Deployment Details

- **System Scale:**
  Hundreds of agents executing trades across multiple markets in real time.
- **Architecture:**
  A decentralized architecture was adopted to eliminate the risks associated with a single point of failure. Agents operated independently but communicated with a central risk management module for oversight.
- **Key Technologies:**
  - **LangGraph Framework:** Provided a robust platform for agent coordination and communication.
  - **Low-Latency Networks:** Ensured rapid data exchange and minimal delay in trade execution.
  - **Machine Learning Integration:** Agents utilized predictive analytics to adjust trading strategies based on market trends.

Challenges Encountered

- **Network Latency:**
  Millisecond-level delays could result in significant financial losses.
- **High Data Throughput:**
  The system had to process vast amounts of real-time market data.
- **Fault Tolerance:**
  Ensuring uninterrupted operation during market volatility was crucial.

Solutions and Lessons Learned

- **Decentralized Control:**
  Eliminating a centralized coordinator minimized latency and enhanced system resilience.
- **Predictive Analytics:**
  Machine learning models were integrated to forecast market trends, enabling agents to make proactive trading decisions.
- **Real-Time Monitoring:**
  Continuous monitoring of system performance and automated alerts allowed for rapid detection and resolution of issues.

Key Takeaways

- **Decentralized architectures** are particularly effective in environments requiring ultra-low latency.
- **Integration of AI and predictive analytics** can significantly enhance decision-making in dynamic markets.
- **Robust real-time monitoring** is essential for maintaining system stability in high-stakes environments.

Summary Table: Case Studies in Scalable LangGraph Deployments

Case Study	Domain	Challenges	Solutions & Lessons Learned
Smart City Traffic Management	Urban Infrastructure	Network latency, centralized bottlenecks, data overload	Decentralized clustering, load balancing, real-time analytics

Case Study	Domain	Challenges	Solutions & Lessons Learned
Industrial IoT in Manufacturing	Manufacturing	Resource contention, synchronization overhead, risk of downtime	Modular design, asynchronous processing, redundancy and failover mechanisms
Distributed Financial Trading System	Financial Services	Ultra-low latency requirements, high data throughput, fault tolerance	Decentralized control, machine learning integration, real-time monitoring

The case studies presented above demonstrate the practical application of LangGraph in diverse, real-world scenarios. Each case study highlights specific scalability challenges such as network latency, resource contention, and synchronization overhead, and details the strategies employed to overcome these issues.

Key lessons learned include:

- **Emphasize decentralization:**
  Distributing control among agents can eliminate central bottlenecks and improve fault tolerance.
- **Implement robust load balancing and asynchronous processing:**
  These techniques are crucial for managing high volumes of data and ensuring timely responses.
- **Integrate predictive analytics and monitoring:**
  Proactive decision-making and continuous system oversight enable rapid adjustments in dynamic environments.

By applying these best practices and learning from real-world examples, you can design and deploy LangGraph-based multi-agent systems that are not only scalable and highly available but also resilient and adaptable to the ever-changing demands of modern applications.

Chapter 10: Performance Optimization Techniques

Optimizing the performance of your LangGraph-based multi-agent system is crucial for ensuring that it operates efficiently, scales effectively, and maintains responsiveness under load. In this chapter, we cover techniques for profiling and benchmarking your system to identify performance bottlenecks, as well as strategies for optimizing agent interactions and communication to reduce latency and overhead.

10.1 Profiling and Benchmarking Your System

Profiling and benchmarking are essential steps in performance optimization. They allow you to measure where time and resources are spent, identify bottlenecks, and quantify improvements as you optimize your system.

Tools and Methodologies for Performance Measurement

Profiling Tools

Profiling tools help you analyze the execution of your code and pinpoint which functions or modules consume the most resources. Some popular Python profiling tools include:

- **cProfile:**
  A built-in Python profiler that provides a detailed report on function call times, call counts, and cumulative times.
- **Py-Spy:**
  A sampling profiler that can profile running Python programs without modifying the code. It is useful for identifying performance issues in production.
- **Line Profiler:**
  Provides detailed information on execution time on a per-line basis, helping to identify inefficient lines within functions.

Benchmarking Tools

Benchmarking involves measuring the performance of specific pieces of code or the system as a whole under defined conditions. Common Python tools for benchmarking include:

- **timeit Module:**
  A standard Python module for timing small bits of Python code. It runs code repeatedly to provide accurate timing measurements.
- **pytest-benchmark:**
  A plugin for the pytest framework that simplifies benchmarking tests and comparing performance across different versions.

Example: Using cProfile and timeit

Below are code examples demonstrating how to use both cProfile and the timeit module for profiling and benchmarking.

Profiling with cProfile

python

```python
# profile_example.py

import cProfile
import pstats

def perform_heavy_computation():
    total = 0
    for i in range(1, 1000000):
        total += i ** 0.5
    return total

if __name__ == "__main__":
    profiler = cProfile.Profile()
    profiler.enable()
    result = perform_heavy_computation()
    profiler.disable()

    print(f"Result of computation: {result}")

    # Create a Stats object and print the top 10 functions by cumulative time
    stats = pstats.Stats(profiler).sort_stats("cumulative")
    stats.print_stats(10)
```

Explanation:

- The perform_heavy_computation() function simulates a CPU-intensive task.
- The cProfile.Profile() object is used to enable profiling before the computation and disable it afterward.
- The pstats.Stats object sorts and prints the top 10 functions by cumulative time, allowing you to identify where most time is spent.

Benchmarking with timeit

python

```
# benchmark_example.py

import timeit

def simple_agent_action():
    # Simulate a simple agent action, e.g., incrementing a counter
    counter = 0
    for i in range(1000):
        counter += 1
    return counter

# Use timeit to measure the execution time of simple_agent_action
execution_time = timeit.timeit("simple_agent_action()", setup="from __main__ import simple_agent_action", number=1000)
print(f"Average execution time over 1000 runs: {execution_time/1000:.6f} seconds")
```

Explanation:

- The simple_agent_action() function simulates a basic operation of an agent.
- The timeit.timeit() function runs this operation 1,000 times and returns the total time taken.
- Dividing the total time by 1,000 gives an average execution time, which helps in assessing performance improvements after optimization.

Methodologies

Micro Benchmarking vs. Macro Benchmarking

- **Micro Benchmarking:**
  Focuses on measuring the performance of small code snippets or individual functions. Useful for optimizing specific parts of your agent code.
- **Macro Benchmarking:**
  Involves testing the performance of the entire system under realistic workloads. This helps in understanding the overall system behavior and the impact of agent interactions, communication delays, and network overhead.

Continuous Monitoring

Implementing continuous monitoring tools, such as Prometheus integrated with Grafana, allows you to track performance metrics (e.g., CPU usage, memory consumption, message latency) in real time. This enables proactive identification and resolution of performance issues in production.

10.2 Optimizing Agent Interactions and Communication

Optimizing how agents interact and communicate is critical for reducing latency and overhead in a distributed multi-agent system. This section outlines strategies and techniques to improve performance in these areas.

Strategies for Reducing Latency

1. **Efficient Messaging Protocols:**
   - **Lightweight Serialization:**
     Use efficient serialization formats like MessagePack or Protocol Buffers instead of verbose formats like JSON or XML.
   - **Batching Messages:**
     Group multiple small messages into a single batch to reduce the overhead associated with network transmissions.
2. **Asynchronous Communication:**
   - **Non-Blocking Operations:**
     Implement asynchronous communication using frameworks

like Python's asyncio to ensure that agents can handle multiple tasks concurrently without waiting for responses.

- o **Event-Driven Architectures:**
  Use event-driven patterns to trigger actions based on specific events rather than continuous polling, thereby reducing unnecessary communication overhead.

3. **Caching and Local Data Storage:**
   - o **In-Memory Caching:**
     Cache frequently accessed data locally within an agent to minimize repeated data retrieval operations.
   - o **Distributed Cache Systems:**
     Use systems like Redis to share cache data across agents, reducing redundant queries to external systems.

Example: Asynchronous Communication in an Agent

Below is an example of an agent that uses asynchronous communication to handle messages without blocking its main task execution.

python

```python
# async_agent.py

import asyncio
from langgraph import Agent

class AsyncAgent(Agent):
    """
    An agent that demonstrates asynchronous communication using asyncio.
    """
    def __init__(self, name):
        super().__init__(name)
        self.task_counter = 0

    async def act(self):
        """
        Asynchronous action method simulating non-blocking task execution.
        """
        self.task_counter += 1
        print(f"{self.name} is performing task #{self.task_counter}")
        # Simulate an asynchronous I/O-bound operation (e.g., a network call)
        await asyncio.sleep(0.5)
```

```python
        print(f"{self.name} completed task #{self.task_counter}")

    async def receive_message(self, message, sender):
        """
        Asynchronous method to handle incoming messages.
        """
        print(f"{self.name} asynchronously received message from
{sender.name}: {message}")
        # Process the message without blocking other operations
        await asyncio.sleep(0.2)
        print(f"{self.name} finished processing message: {message}")

# Example usage of AsyncAgent
async def main():
    agent = AsyncAgent("Async Agent")

    # Run act() and receive_message() concurrently
    await asyncio.gather(
        agent.act(),
        agent.receive_message("Hello, Async Agent!", agent)
    )

if __name__ == "__main__":
    asyncio.run(main())
```

Explanation:

- **Asynchronous Methods:**
  The act() and receive_message() methods are defined as
  asynchronous functions using the async def syntax. This allows them
  to run concurrently without blocking.
- **Simulated I/O Operations:**
  await asyncio.sleep() simulates I/O-bound operations, such as
  network requests, demonstrating how agents can remain responsive
  while waiting for external events.
- **Concurrency with asyncio.gather():**
  The asyncio.gather() function is used in the main() function to run
  both actions concurrently, showcasing efficient parallel processing
  within the agent.

Optimizing Communication Overhead

1. **Reducing Redundancy:**
   - **Selective Broadcasting:**
     Instead of broadcasting every message to all agents, design a mechanism for targeted or selective message dissemination.
   - **Message Filtering:**
     Allow agents to subscribe to specific types of messages to avoid processing irrelevant data.
2. **Optimizing Network Protocols:**
   - **TCP vs. UDP:**
     Choose the appropriate network protocol based on the required reliability and latency. For example, UDP may be used for real-time data where occasional packet loss is acceptable, while TCP is preferred for critical communications.
   - **Compression:**
     Compress data before transmission to reduce network load, especially for large payloads.

Summary Table: Strategies for Reducing Latency and Overhead

Strategy	Technique	Benefits	Example
Efficient Messaging	Lightweight serialization, message batching	Reduced transmission time and network load	Using MessagePack instead of JSON
Asynchronous Communication	Non-blocking operations, event-driven architectures	Improved responsiveness, concurrent processing	Using asyncio to manage agent actions concurrently
Caching	In-memory caching, distributed caches	Reduced redundant data retrieval	Using Redis to cache frequent data
Selective Communication	Targeted broadcasting, message filtering	Lower communication overhead, reduced processing load	Agents subscribe only to relevant event types

Performance optimization in a multi-agent system is an ongoing process that requires careful measurement, analysis, and iterative improvements. In this chapter, we covered essential techniques for profiling and benchmarking your LangGraph-based system using tools like cProfile and timeit. We discussed methodologies for both micro and macro benchmarking, emphasizing the importance of continuous monitoring.

We then explored strategies for optimizing agent interactions and communication. By implementing asynchronous communication, efficient messaging protocols, and caching mechanisms, you can significantly reduce latency and overhead, leading to a more responsive and scalable system.

The provided examples and summary tables illustrate how to apply these techniques in practice. By adopting these performance optimization practices, you will be better equipped to ensure that your multi-agent system not only meets current performance requirements but is also prepared to scale and adapt to future demands in complex, distributed environments.

10.3 Load Balancing and Concurrency Management

Load balancing and concurrency management are key to ensuring that the system distributes tasks evenly among agents and makes efficient use of available processing power. This section discusses various techniques for distributing workloads evenly, managing concurrent operations, and minimizing latency and overhead.

Techniques for Distributing Workloads Evenly

1. Round-Robin Scheduling

Round-robin scheduling is one of the simplest methods for load balancing. Tasks are assigned to agents sequentially in a cyclic order. This approach is effective when all agents have roughly equal processing capabilities.

Example: Round-Robin Task Distribution

python

round_robin_scheduler.py

```python
from langgraph import Agent, GraphSystem

class WorkerAgent(Agent):
    """
    An agent that processes tasks.
    """

    def __init__(self, name):
        super().__init__(name)

    def process_task(self, task):
        """
        Simulate task processing.
        """

        print(f"{self.name} is processing task: {task}")

def round_robin_scheduler(agents, tasks):
    """
    Distribute tasks among agents using round-robin scheduling.

    Parameters:
    - agents: List of WorkerAgent instances.
    - tasks: List of tasks to be processed.
    """
    num_agents = len(agents)
    for index, task in enumerate(tasks):
        agent = agents[index % num_agents]
        agent.process_task(task)

# Example usage:
if __name__ == "__main__":
    # Create a LangGraph system (for context)
    system = GraphSystem()

    # Instantiate WorkerAgents
    agents = [WorkerAgent(f"Agent_{i}") for i in range(1, 4)]
    for agent in agents:
        system.add_agent(agent)

    # Define a list of tasks
    tasks = [f"Task_{i}" for i in range(1, 10)]

    # Distribute tasks using round-robin scheduling
```

```
round_robin_scheduler(agents, tasks)
```

Explanation:

- **Agent Definition:**
  The WorkerAgent class extends the LangGraph Agent class and defines a process_task() method to simulate processing a task.
- **Round-Robin Scheduler:**
  The round_robin_scheduler() function distributes tasks evenly across agents by assigning each task to an agent based on the task index modulo the number of agents.
- **System Context:**
  The example creates a simple LangGraph system, adds agents, and then distributes a list of tasks among them.

2. Weighted Distribution

In environments where agents have different capacities, weighted distribution is more appropriate. Each agent is assigned a weight based on its processing power, and tasks are distributed proportionally.

Conceptual Example:

Imagine three agents with weights 2, 1, and 1 respectively. For 8 tasks, the agent with weight 2 should receive 4 tasks while the others receive 2 each.

3. Dynamic Scheduling

Dynamic scheduling adapts task distribution based on real-time performance metrics. Agents can signal their current load or processing speed, and a scheduler can use this information to assign tasks more effectively. Techniques such as adaptive load balancing and work stealing are common in high-performance computing.

Concurrency Management

Concurrency management involves handling multiple tasks simultaneously without blocking operations. This can be achieved using:

1. Asynchronous Programming

Using asynchronous programming frameworks (like Python's asyncio) allows agents to perform I/O-bound tasks concurrently without waiting for each operation to complete.

Example: Asynchronous Agent Operations

python

```python
# async_worker_agent.py

import asyncio
from langgraph import Agent

class AsyncWorkerAgent(Agent):
    """
    An agent that processes tasks asynchronously.
    """
    def __init__(self, name):
        super().__init__(name)
        self.task_count = 0

    async def process_task(self, task):
        """
        Asynchronously process a task.
        """
        self.task_count += 1
        print(f"{self.name} is starting task: {task}")
        # Simulate an asynchronous I/O-bound operation
        await asyncio.sleep(0.5)
        print(f"{self.name} completed task: {task}")

async def main():
    # Create an instance of AsyncWorkerAgent
    agent = AsyncWorkerAgent("AsyncAgent")
    tasks = [f"Task_{i}" for i in range(1, 6)]
    # Process tasks concurrently
    await asyncio.gather(*(agent.process_task(task) for task in tasks))

if __name__ == "__main__":
    asyncio.run(main())
```

Explanation:

- **AsyncWorkerAgent:**
  This agent processes tasks asynchronously using the async def syntax and await statements to simulate non-blocking operations.
- **Concurrency with asyncio.gather():**
  The main() function demonstrates concurrent task execution, ensuring the agent processes multiple tasks efficiently without blocking.

2. Multithreading and Multiprocessing

For CPU-bound tasks, multithreading or multiprocessing can help distribute the workload across multiple cores. Python's concurrent.futures module provides a simple interface for both.

Summary Table: Load Balancing and Concurrency Strategies

Strategy	Technique	Benefits	Example
Round-Robin Scheduling	Sequential distribution of tasks	Simple and effective for equal-capacity agents	Code example above
Weighted Distribution	Task allocation based on agent capacity	Balances load among heterogeneous agents	Conceptual, implemented with weights
Dynamic Scheduling	Real-time adaptation using performance metrics	Maximizes efficiency under variable loads	Adaptive algorithms, work stealing
Asynchronous Programming	Non-blocking I/O with asyncio	Improves responsiveness for I/O-bound tasks	Async example above
Multithreading/Multiprocessing	Concurrent task execution	Enhances performance for CPU-bound tasks	concurrent.futures module

Strategy	Technique	Benefits	Example
	on multiple cores		

10.4 Resource Management and Memory Optimization

Efficient resource management and memory optimization are critical for ensuring that a multi-agent system operates smoothly, especially as the system scales. This section outlines strategies for managing computational resources effectively and optimizing memory usage.

Strategies for Efficient Use of Computational Resources

1. Resource Monitoring and Profiling

- **Monitoring Tools:**
  Utilize system monitoring tools (e.g., Prometheus, Grafana) to track CPU, memory, and I/O usage in real time.
- **Profiling:**
  Use profiling tools (e.g., cProfile, Py-Spy) to identify resource-intensive parts of your code and optimize them.

2. Caching Mechanisms

Caching reduces redundant computations and data retrieval. Implementing in-memory caches using tools like Redis or Python dictionaries can significantly improve performance.

Example: Simple Caching with a Dictionary

python

```
# caching_example.py

cache = {}

def compute_expensive_operation(x):
    """
    Simulate an expensive computation.
    """
```

```
# If the result is cached, return it directly
if x in cache:
    print(f"Retrieving cached result for {x}")
    return cache[x]

# Otherwise, compute and cache the result
result = x ** 2  # Replace with a more complex computation if needed
cache[x] = result
print(f"Caching result for {x}: {result}")
return result

# Example usage:
for i in [10, 20, 10, 30, 20]:
    print(f"Result: {compute_expensive_operation(i)}")
```

Explanation:

- **Cache Lookup:**
  The function first checks if the result for a given input is already cached.
- **Result Caching:**
  If not cached, it computes the result, stores it in the cache, and then returns it.
- **Benefit:**
  Repeated operations with the same input are served from the cache, reducing computational overhead.

3. Efficient Data Structures

Choosing the right data structures is crucial for optimizing performance and memory usage. For example:

- **Lists vs. Tuples:**
  Tuples are immutable and generally use less memory than lists.
- **Sets and Dictionaries:**
  For membership testing, sets and dictionaries provide average $O(1)$ time complexity, which is faster than lists.

4. Memory Management Techniques

- **Garbage Collection:**
  Python's garbage collector automatically frees unused memory.

However, explicitly managing resources with context managers (using with statements) can further improve memory usage.

- **Memory Pools and Object Reuse:**
  Reuse objects where possible instead of creating new ones repeatedly, which can help reduce memory fragmentation.

Example: Using a Context Manager for Resource Management

python

```python
# file_processing.py

def process_file(file_path):
    """
    Process a file using a context manager to ensure it is properly closed.
    """
    with open(file_path, 'r') as file:
        data = file.read()
        # Process data (e.g., parsing, analysis)
        print(f"Processed data from {file_path}")

# Example usage:
if __name__ == "__main__":
    process_file("example.txt")
```

Explanation:

- **Context Manager:**
  The with open(...) statement ensures that the file is automatically closed after processing, which helps manage system resources efficiently.

Summary Table: Resource Management and Memory Optimization Strategies

Strategy	Technique	Benefits	Example
Resource Monitoring	Use tools like Prometheus and Grafana	Real-time tracking of CPU, memory, and I/O usage	System dashboards

Strategy	Technique	Benefits	Example
Profiling	Tools such as cProfile, Py-Spy	Identify and optimize resource-intensive code sections	cProfile example
Caching	In-memory caching with Redis or dictionaries	Reduces redundant computations and speeds up data retrieval	Caching example above
Efficient Data Structures	Use tuples, sets, dictionaries	Faster operations and reduced memory usage	Choosing the appropriate Python data type
Garbage Collection & Context Managers	Use with statements for automatic resource cleanup	Ensures proper resource management and minimizes memory leaks	File processing example
Object Reuse	Memory pooling and reusing objects	Reduces overhead from frequent object creation	Custom object pooling strategies

Performance optimization in multi-agent systems requires a multifaceted approach. In this chapter, we explored techniques for load balancing and concurrency management to distribute workloads evenly and reduce processing latency. We also discussed strategies for resource management and memory optimization, emphasizing the importance of monitoring, caching, efficient data structures, and proper memory management practices.

By employing these strategies and utilizing the provided code examples and summary tables, you can significantly enhance the performance and scalability of your LangGraph-based systems. These techniques ensure that your system not only meets current demands but is also well-prepared for future growth and increased workload, resulting in a robust, efficient, and high-performing multi-agent environment.

Chapter 11: Cloud Deployment and Distributed Architectures

Deploying multi-agent systems in the cloud and leveraging distributed architectures can significantly enhance scalability, flexibility, and resilience. In this chapter, we will provide an overview of major cloud platforms and their service offerings and discuss containerization and orchestration techniques—specifically Docker, Kubernetes, and microservices architecture—that are essential for modern cloud deployments.

11.1 Overview of Cloud Platforms and Services

Cloud platforms offer a wide range of services that simplify the deployment, scaling, and management of distributed systems. They provide computing resources on-demand, eliminating the need for expensive on-premise infrastructure and enabling rapid scaling based on workload requirements.

Major Cloud Providers and Their Offerings

Several major cloud providers dominate the market, each offering a comprehensive suite of services. Below is an overview of some of the most prominent providers:

1. Amazon Web Services (AWS)

Key Offerings:

- **Compute:**
  - *Amazon EC2:* Virtual servers with flexible configurations.
  - *AWS Lambda:* Serverless computing for running code in response to events.
- **Storage:**
  - *Amazon S3:* Scalable object storage.
  - *Amazon EBS:* Block storage for EC2 instances.
- **Networking:**
  - *Amazon VPC:* Virtual Private Cloud for isolated network environments.
- **Managed Services:**

- o *Amazon RDS:* Managed relational database service.
- o *Amazon ECS/EKS:* Container orchestration using Docker (ECS) and Kubernetes (EKS).

2. Microsoft Azure

Key Offerings:

- **Compute:**
  - o *Azure Virtual Machines:* On-demand scalable computing.
  - o *Azure Functions:* Serverless computing.
- **Storage:**
  - o *Azure Blob Storage:* Unstructured object storage.
  - o *Azure Disk Storage:* Managed disks for VMs.
- **Networking:**
  - o *Azure Virtual Network:* Isolated network environments.
- **Managed Services:**
  - o *Azure SQL Database:* Managed relational database service.
  - o *Azure Kubernetes Service (AKS):* Managed Kubernetes cluster for container orchestration.

3. Google Cloud Platform (GCP)

Key Offerings:

- **Compute:**
  - o *Google Compute Engine:* Virtual machines with custom configurations.
  - o *Google Cloud Functions:* Serverless computing.
- **Storage:**
  - o *Google Cloud Storage:* Highly durable and scalable object storage.
  - o *Persistent Disks:* Block storage for VMs.
- **Networking:**
  - o *Virtual Private Cloud (VPC):* Network isolation and configuration.
- **Managed Services:**
  - o *Cloud SQL:* Managed relational databases.
  - o *Google Kubernetes Engine (GKE):* Managed Kubernetes for container orchestration.

Comparison Table: Major Cloud Providers

Provider	Compute Services	Storage Services	Networking	Container Orchestration
AWS	EC2, Lambda	S3, EBS	VPC	ECS, EKS
Azure	Virtual Machines, Functions	Blob Storage, Disk Storage	Virtual Network	AKS
GCP	Compute Engine, Cloud Functions	Cloud Storage, Persistent Disks	VPC	GKE

Cloud Service Benefits for Multi-Agent Systems

- **Scalability:**
  Cloud platforms provide the ability to scale resources up or down based on demand, ensuring that your multi-agent system can handle peak loads and grow over time.
- **Cost Efficiency:**
  Pay-as-you-go pricing models help reduce capital expenditure, as you only pay for the resources you use.
- **High Availability and Resilience:**
  Cloud providers offer built-in redundancy, geographic distribution, and robust disaster recovery solutions.
- **Managed Services:**
  Managed databases, container orchestration, and serverless computing allow you to focus on application logic rather than infrastructure management.

11.2 Containerization and Orchestration

Containerization has revolutionized application deployment by providing a consistent and isolated environment for software execution. Orchestration platforms like Kubernetes manage the lifecycle of containers, ensuring that applications are deployed, scaled, and maintained effectively.

Containerization with Docker

What is Docker?
Docker is a popular containerization platform that packages applications and

their dependencies into containers. These containers are lightweight, portable, and ensure consistency across development, testing, and production environments.

Example: Dockerfile for a LangGraph Agent

Below is an example of a simple Dockerfile to containerize a LangGraph agent application.

dockerfile

```
# Use an official Python runtime as a parent image
FROM python:3.9-slim

# Set the working directory in the container
WORKDIR /app

# Copy the current directory contents into the container at /app
COPY . /app

# Install any needed packages specified in requirements.txt
RUN pip install --no-cache-dir -r requirements.txt

# Make port 8000 available to the world outside this container
EXPOSE 8000

# Define environment variable
ENV LANGGRAPH_ENV=production

# Run the LangGraph agent application when the container launches
CMD ["python", "run_langgraph.py"]
```

Explanation:

- **Base Image:**
  The image starts with the official Python 3.9 slim image.
- **Working Directory:**
  Sets the working directory to /app.
- **Copying Files:**
  Copies the application code into the container.
- **Installing Dependencies:**
  Installs required Python packages.

- **Port Exposure:**
  Exposes port 8000 for network communication.
- **Environment Variables and Command:**
  Sets an environment variable and defines the command to run the application.

Orchestration with Kubernetes

What is Kubernetes?
Kubernetes is an open-source container orchestration platform that automates the deployment, scaling, and management of containerized applications. It provides robust features such as load balancing, service discovery, self-healing, and automated rollouts and rollbacks.

Example: Kubernetes Deployment YAML for a LangGraph Agent

Below is an example of a Kubernetes deployment file to deploy a LangGraph agent container.

yaml

```yaml
apiVersion: apps/v1
kind: Deployment
metadata:
  name: langgraph-agent-deployment
spec:
  replicas: 3
  selector:
    matchLabels:
      app: langgraph-agent
  template:
    metadata:
      labels:
        app: langgraph-agent
    spec:
      containers:
      - name: langgraph-agent
        image: your-docker-repo/langgraph-agent:latest
        ports:
        - containerPort: 8000
        env:
        - name: LANGGRAPH_ENV
```

```
          value: "production"
---
apiVersion: v1
kind: Service
metadata:
  name: langgraph-agent-service
spec:
  type: LoadBalancer
  selector:
    app: langgraph-agent
  ports:
   - protocol: TCP
     port: 80
     targetPort: 8000
```

Explanation:

- **Deployment:**
  Defines a deployment for the LangGraph agent with three replicas to ensure high availability and load balancing.
- **Template and Containers:**
  Specifies the container image, port configuration, and environment variables.
- **Service:**
  Exposes the deployment through a LoadBalancer service, making the agents accessible via port 80.

Microservices Architecture

What is Microservices Architecture?
Microservices architecture is an approach to building applications as a collection of loosely coupled, independently deployable services. In a multi-agent system, each agent or group of agents can be considered a microservice that performs a specific function.

Benefits:

- **Scalability:**
  Individual services can be scaled independently based on demand.
- **Resilience:**
  Failure in one service does not necessarily impact others.

- **Flexibility:**
  Services can be developed, deployed, and updated independently.

Comparison Table: Containerization and Orchestration

Aspect	Docker (Containerization)	Kubernetes (Orchestration)
Purpose	Package applications with their dependencies	Automate deployment, scaling, and management of containers
Key Benefits	Portability, consistency, lightweight	Self-healing, load balancing, service discovery, scalability
Core Components	Docker images, containers	Pods, Deployments, Services, ReplicaSets
Deployment Example	Dockerfile for LangGraph agent	Kubernetes YAML for deploying multiple replicas

Summary

- **Containerization** with Docker enables you to package your LangGraph agent application into a portable, consistent environment.
- **Orchestration** with Kubernetes automates the deployment, scaling, and management of these containers, ensuring high availability and resilience.
- **Microservices Architecture** allows you to break down your application into independent components that can be developed and scaled independently.

Deploying multi-agent systems in the cloud using modern containerization and orchestration technologies offers significant benefits in terms of scalability, flexibility, and high availability. In this chapter, we provided a detailed overview of major cloud platforms such as AWS, Azure, and GCP, and discussed their key service offerings that support multi-agent systems. We then explored the role of containerization with Docker and orchestration with Kubernetes, including practical examples and configuration files to guide you through the deployment process.

By leveraging these technologies, you can build robust, scalable, and resilient multi-agent systems that are well-suited for dynamic and demanding environments. Whether you are deploying in a public cloud or a hybrid environment, these cloud deployment strategies and distributed architectures will empower your LangGraph-based systems to achieve optimal performance and flexibility.

11.3 Deploying LangGraph in a Distributed Environment

Deploying LangGraph in a distributed environment involves more than simply running your multi-agent system on multiple servers. It requires careful planning to ensure that the system is scalable, resilient, and performs well under varying loads. In this section, we discuss best practices for deploying LangGraph in such environments and strategies to scale your system effectively.

Best Practices for Deployment and Scaling

1. Design for Scalability

- **Modular Architecture:**
  Ensure that your LangGraph-based system is designed as a collection of loosely coupled modules. This allows you to scale individual components independently based on their load and performance characteristics.
- **Decentralized Control:**
  Avoid single points of failure by distributing control functions. Use decentralized architectures where possible to improve resilience and reduce latency.
- **Service Partitioning:**
  Partition your agent network into clusters or groups based on functionality or geographical location. This segmentation can help in reducing communication overhead and improving response times.

2. Use Containerization and Orchestration

- **Containerization:**
  Package your LangGraph agents and services into containers using Docker. Containers encapsulate all dependencies, ensuring consistency across development, testing, and production environments.

- **Orchestration with Kubernetes:**
  Deploy your containers using orchestration platforms like Kubernetes, which provide automated scaling, load balancing, and self-healing capabilities.

Example: Kubernetes Deployment YAML for LangGraph Agents

yaml

```yaml
apiVersion: apps/v1
kind: Deployment
metadata:
  name: langgraph-agent-deployment
spec:
  replicas: 5
  selector:
    matchLabels:
      app: langgraph-agent
  template:
    metadata:
      labels:
        app: langgraph-agent
    spec:
      containers:
      - name: langgraph-agent
        image: your-docker-repo/langgraph-agent:latest
        ports:
        - containerPort: 8000
        env:
        - name: LANGGRAPH_ENV
          value: "production"
---
apiVersion: v1
kind: Service
metadata:
  name: langgraph-agent-service
spec:
  type: LoadBalancer
  selector:
    app: langgraph-agent
  ports:
```

```
    - protocol: TCP
      port: 80
      targetPort: 8000
```

Explanation:
This YAML file deploys five replicas of your LangGraph agent
container. It uses a LoadBalancer service to distribute incoming
traffic, ensuring that requests are balanced across all available agents.

3. Implement Auto-Scaling and Load Balancing

- **Auto-Scaling:**
  Configure auto-scaling policies based on metrics such as CPU usage,
  memory consumption, or network latency. For example, Kubernetes
  supports Horizontal Pod Autoscaling (HPA) to dynamically adjust
  the number of replicas.
- **Load Balancing:**
  Use load balancing solutions to evenly distribute workload among
  agents. This can be achieved through cloud-native load balancers
  (e.g., AWS ELB, Azure Load Balancer) or by using built-in
  Kubernetes services.

4. Monitoring and Logging

- **Real-Time Monitoring:**
  Implement monitoring tools such as Prometheus and Grafana to
  visualize performance metrics and track system health in real time.
- **Centralized Logging:**
  Use centralized logging solutions (e.g., ELK Stack, Splunk) to
  aggregate logs from all agents. This simplifies debugging and
  performance analysis across distributed components.

11.4 CI/CD and Automated Deployment Pipelines

Continuous Integration and Continuous Deployment (CI/CD) pipelines are
essential for maintaining high-quality code and automating the deployment
process. These practices help ensure that new code changes are tested,
integrated, and deployed with minimal manual intervention.

Tools and Techniques for Continuous Integration

1. CI/CD Pipeline Tools

- **Jenkins:**
  A widely used automation server that supports a multitude of plugins for building, testing, and deploying applications.
- **GitLab CI/CD:**
  Integrated within GitLab, this tool allows you to define your CI/CD pipelines using YAML configuration files.
- **GitHub Actions:**
  A flexible automation tool integrated with GitHub repositories, enabling workflows for building, testing, and deploying code.
- **CircleCI:**
  A cloud-based CI/CD platform that offers fast and scalable pipelines.

2. Automated Testing and Deployment

- **Automated Testing:**
  Integrate unit, integration, and end-to-end tests into your pipeline to catch issues early. Use frameworks such as pytest for Python applications.
- **Automated Builds:**
  Automate the build process to create container images, ensuring that the environment is consistent and reproducible.
- **Deployment Automation:**
  Automate the deployment process using scripts and tools like Helm (for Kubernetes) to manage release configurations.

Example: GitLab CI/CD Pipeline Configuration

Below is an example of a .gitlab-ci.yml file for automating the build and deployment of a LangGraph-based system.

yaml

```
stages:
  - build
  - test
  - deploy

build:
  stage: build
  image: docker:latest
```

```yaml
  services:
    - docker:dind
  script:
    - docker build -t your-docker-repo/langgraph-
agent:$CI_COMMIT_SHORT_SHA .
    - docker push your-docker-repo/langgraph-
agent:$CI_COMMIT_SHORT_SHA
  only:
    - master

test:
  stage: test
  image: python:3.9-slim
  script:
    - pip install -r requirements.txt
    - pytest
  only:
    - master

deploy:
  stage: deploy
  image: bitnami/kubectl:latest
  script:
    - kubectl set image deployment/langgraph-agent-deployment langgraph-
agent=your-docker-repo/langgraph-agent:$CI_COMMIT_SHORT_SHA
  only:
    - master
```

Explanation:

- **Stages:**
  The pipeline is divided into build, test, and deploy stages.
- **Build Stage:**
  Uses Docker to build and push the container image.
- **Test Stage:**
  Installs dependencies and runs tests using pytest.
- **Deploy Stage:**
  Uses kubectl to update the deployment with the new image version.
- **Branch Filtering:**
  The pipeline runs only on the master branch to ensure that only stable
  code is deployed.

11.5 Security, Compliance, and Maintenance in the Cloud

Deploying multi-agent systems in the cloud necessitates rigorous attention to security, compliance, and ongoing maintenance. Ensuring data protection and adhering to regulatory standards are paramount for maintaining trust and operational integrity.

Ensuring Data Protection and Regulatory Adherence

1. Security Best Practices

- **Encryption:**
  - **In-Transit Encryption:**
    Use TLS/SSL for all communications between agents and external systems.
  - **At-Rest Encryption:**
    Encrypt data stored in databases, file systems, and cloud storage solutions.
- **Access Control:**
  - **Authentication and Authorization:**
    Implement robust access control mechanisms using IAM (Identity and Access Management) services provided by cloud platforms (e.g., AWS IAM, Azure AD).
  - **Role-Based Access Control (RBAC):**
    Use RBAC to restrict access to sensitive resources based on user roles.
- **Network Security:**
  - **Firewalls and VPCs:**
    Use Virtual Private Clouds (VPCs), security groups, and firewalls to isolate and protect network traffic.
  - **Regular Security Audits:**
    Perform vulnerability assessments and penetration testing to identify and mitigate security risks.

2. Compliance and Regulatory Adherence

- **Compliance Frameworks:**
  Ensure that your deployment complies with relevant regulatory standards such as GDPR, HIPAA, or PCI-DSS, depending on your industry.

- **Data Governance:**
  Implement data governance policies that define data handling, storage, and access procedures. Regular audits and compliance checks should be part of your maintenance strategy.
- **Documentation and Reporting:**
  Maintain comprehensive documentation of your security measures, compliance policies, and incident response plans. Automated reporting tools can help track compliance status and generate audit reports.

3. Maintenance and Continuous Improvement

- **Automated Patch Management:**
  Use automated tools to apply security patches and updates to your operating systems, applications, and container images.
- **Monitoring and Alerts:**
  Continuously monitor system logs, network traffic, and application performance. Set up automated alerts to notify administrators of any suspicious activities or performance anomalies.
- **Backup and Disaster Recovery:**
  Implement robust backup solutions and disaster recovery plans to ensure that data can be restored in case of a failure or security breach.

Example: AWS IAM Policy for LangGraph Deployment

Below is an example of an AWS IAM policy that restricts access to LangGraph resources, ensuring that only authorized users can perform sensitive operations.

json

```json
{
  "Version": "2012-10-17",
  "Statement": [
    {
      "Sid": "LangGraphAccess",
      "Effect": "Allow",
      "Action": [
        "ec2:DescribeInstances",
        "ecs:DescribeClusters",
        "ecs:ListTasks",
        "ecs:DescribeTasks",
```

```
      "ecr:GetDownloadUrlForLayer",
      "ecr:BatchGetImage"
    ],
    "Resource": "*"
  },
  {
    "Sid": "RestrictedActions",
    "Effect": "Deny",
    "Action": [
      "ec2:TerminateInstances",
      "ecs:DeleteCluster"
    ],
    "Resource": "*"
  }
 ]
}
```

Explanation:

- **Allow Statement:**
  Grants permissions to view and describe resources necessary for
  operating LangGraph, such as EC2 instances and ECS clusters.
- **Deny Statement:**
  Explicitly denies high-risk actions like terminating instances or
  deleting clusters, providing an additional layer of protection.

Summary Table: Cloud Security and Compliance Best Practices

Aspect	Best Practices	Benefits
Encryption	TLS/SSL for in-transit; AES for at-rest	Protects data confidentiality and integrity
Access Control	Use IAM, RBAC, MFA (Multi-Factor Authentication)	Restricts unauthorized access; enhances accountability
Network Security	VPCs, security groups, firewalls, VPNs	Isolates and secures network traffic
Compliance	Adhere to GDPR, HIPAA, PCI-DSS; perform regular audits and compliance checks	Ensures regulatory adherence and builds customer trust

Aspect	Best Practices	Benefits
Maintenance	Automated patch management, continuous monitoring, backup, and disaster recovery	Minimizes downtime; ensures rapid recovery from incidents

Deploying LangGraph in a distributed cloud environment, establishing robust CI/CD pipelines, and ensuring stringent security and compliance measures are critical components for a successful production-grade multi-agent system. In this section, we discussed best practices for deploying and scaling LangGraph across distributed environments, provided practical examples of CI/CD pipeline configurations, and outlined essential strategies for maintaining security, compliance, and data integrity in the cloud.

By leveraging these techniques and tools, you can achieve automated, reliable, and secure deployments that are well-suited to the dynamic demands of modern, distributed multi-agent systems. These strategies not only streamline deployment and maintenance processes but also provide the foundation for continuous improvement and operational excellence.

Chapter 12: Practical Applications of LangGraph

LangGraph is a versatile framework that can be applied to a wide range of real-world domains. In this chapter, we explore two practical applications: autonomous robotics and IoT systems, and financial services with algorithmic trading. Each section demonstrates how LangGraph can be used to design, deploy, and manage complex, distributed, real-time systems that are responsive, adaptive, and scalable.

12.1 Autonomous Robotics and IoT Systems

Autonomous robotics and IoT systems are at the forefront of modern technology, requiring rapid, responsive, and adaptive control mechanisms. These systems combine physical robots, smart sensors, and connected devices to create environments that can react intelligently to changes. LangGraph offers a powerful means to coordinate and manage the interactions between multiple autonomous agents in such scenarios.

Designing Responsive and Adaptive Robotic Systems

When designing robotic and IoT systems, the following factors are crucial:

- **Real-Time Responsiveness:**
  Agents must process sensor data and make decisions in real time. This is essential for applications such as autonomous navigation, obstacle avoidance, and environmental monitoring.
- **Adaptive Behavior:**
  Robots and IoT devices often operate in dynamic environments. They need to adapt to changes such as varying sensor inputs, changing environmental conditions, or unexpected obstacles.
- **Distributed Coordination:**
  In multi-robot systems, or when integrating various IoT devices, coordination among agents is vital. Agents must share information, collaborate on tasks, and adjust their actions based on collective input.

- **Robust Communication:**
  Reliable, low-latency communication channels are critical to ensure that data is shared promptly and decisions are made accurately.

LangGraph in Robotics and IoT

LangGraph facilitates these requirements through its graph-based modeling of agents and interactions. Each robot or sensor can be represented as a node, while the communication channels between them are modeled as edges. This allows system designers to:

- Visualize the overall network topology.
- Implement dynamic updates as devices join or leave the network.
- Optimize communication paths to reduce latency.

Example: Simulating a Robotic Agent Receiving Sensor Data

Below is a simplified Python example that simulates a robotic agent which monitors sensor data from an IoT device and adjusts its behavior accordingly. In this example, the agent changes its operational mode based on the temperature data received.

python

```python
# robotics_agent.py

import asyncio
import random
from langgraph import Agent

class RoboticAgent(Agent):
    """
    A robotic agent that adapts its behavior based on sensor data.
    """
    def __init__(self, name):
        super().__init__(name)
        self.mode = "normal"  # Possible modes: normal, cooling, alert

    async def monitor_sensors(self):
        """
        Asynchronously monitor sensor data (e.g., temperature) and adjust
behavior.
```

```python
    """
    while True:
        # Simulate receiving temperature data from a sensor
        temperature = random.uniform(20.0, 80.0)  # Temperature in Celsius
        print(f"{self.name} received temperature: {temperature:.2f}°C")
        self.adjust_behavior(temperature)
        # Wait for 2 seconds before reading the sensor again
        await asyncio.sleep(2)

def adjust_behavior(self, temperature):
    """
    Adjust the agent's operational mode based on temperature.
    """
    if temperature > 60:
        self.mode = "cooling"
    elif temperature > 75:
        self.mode = "alert"
    else:
        self.mode = "normal"
    print(f"{self.name} set mode to: {self.mode}")

# Example usage:
async def main():
    agent = RoboticAgent("Robot_1")
    # Run the sensor monitoring task indefinitely
    await agent.monitor_sensors()

if __name__ == "__main__":
    asyncio.run(main())
```

Explanation:

- **Asynchronous Sensor Monitoring:**
  The monitor_sensors() method simulates periodic sensor readings using asyncio.sleep(), ensuring non-blocking operations.
- **Behavior Adjustment:**
  The adjust_behavior() method changes the agent's mode based on the received temperature, demonstrating adaptive decision-making.
- **Real-Time Simulation:**
  The agent continuously monitors sensor data and adjusts its operation, a typical requirement in autonomous robotic and IoT systems.

Benefits and Challenges

Aspect	Benefits	Challenges
Real-Time Responsiveness	Quick adaptation to sensor data for timely decisions.	Ensuring low-latency communication across distributed agents.
Adaptive Behavior	Agents can autonomously adjust to environmental changes.	Complex decision-making in highly dynamic environments.
Distributed Coordination	Enhanced collaboration between multiple robots or sensors.	Managing communication overhead and ensuring data consistency.
Robustness	Graph-based modeling simplifies the management of dynamic networks.	Handling failures and intermittent connectivity.

12.2 Financial Services and Algorithmic Trading

Financial services, particularly algorithmic trading, demand real-time decision-making systems that can process vast amounts of market data and execute trades with minimal latency. LangGraph can be applied in these environments to coordinate trading agents, analyze market trends, and implement real-time strategies.

Implementing Real-Time Decision Systems in Finance

Key requirements in algorithmic trading include:

- **Low Latency Processing:**
  Trading systems must process market data and execute trades in milliseconds to capitalize on fleeting opportunities.
- **High Throughput:**
  The system must handle a high volume of data from various market feeds and process multiple transactions concurrently.
- **Fault Tolerance:**
  The system should maintain operation even if individual agents fail, ensuring continuous trading during critical periods.
- **Predictive Analytics:**
  Incorporating machine learning models can enhance decision-making

by forecasting market trends and adjusting trading strategies dynamically.

LangGraph in Algorithmic Trading

Using LangGraph, trading agents can be modeled as nodes in a graph, with edges representing communication channels through which market data, trading signals, and risk assessments are shared. This approach allows for:

- **Decentralized Decision-Making:**
  Trading agents can make independent decisions based on localized market data, reducing the risk of bottlenecks.
- **Collaboration:**
  Agents can share information about market trends and coordinate strategies to optimize trade execution.
- **Resilience:**
  The distributed nature of LangGraph helps ensure that the overall system remains robust even if some agents encounter issues.

Example: A Simple Trading Agent Simulation

Below is an example of a trading agent that processes simulated market data and makes buy or sell decisions based on simple thresholds. This example demonstrates real-time decision-making in a distributed trading environment.

python

```python
# trading_agent.py

import asyncio
import random
from langgraph import Agent

class TradingAgent(Agent):
    """
    A trading agent that simulates real-time market decision-making.
    """
    def __init__(self, name):
        super().__init__(name)
        self.position = "neutral"  # Possible positions: neutral, long, short

    async def monitor_market(self):
```

```python
    """
    Asynchronously monitor market data and make trading decisions.
    """
    while True:
        # Simulate receiving market data (e.g., stock price)
        price = random.uniform(90.0, 110.0)
        print(f"{self.name} observed market price: ${price:.2f}")
        self.decide_trade(price)
        # Wait for 1 second before checking the market again
        await asyncio.sleep(1)

    def decide_trade(self, price):
        """
        Make a trading decision based on the current market price.
        """
        if price < 95:
            self.position = "long"  # Buy signal
            print(f"{self.name} decision: BUY at ${price:.2f}")
        elif price > 105:
            self.position = "short"  # Sell signal
            print(f"{self.name} decision: SELL at ${price:.2f}")
        else:
            self.position = "neutral"  # Hold position
            print(f"{self.name} decision: HOLD at ${price:.2f}")

# Example usage:
async def main():
    trader = TradingAgent("Trader_1")
    # Run the market monitoring task indefinitely
    await trader.monitor_market()

if __name__ == "__main__":
    asyncio.run(main())
```

Explanation:

- **Real-Time Market Monitoring:**
  The monitor_market() method simulates the continuous reception of market data using asynchronous operations.
- **Trading Decision Logic:**
  The decide_trade() method uses simple threshold conditions to decide whether to buy, sell, or hold a position. In a real system, this

logic could be enhanced with machine learning models and more complex criteria.

- **Continuous Operation:**
  The asynchronous design ensures that the agent can process market data in real time without blocking, which is critical for algorithmic trading.

Benefits and Challenges in Financial Systems

Aspect	Benefits	Challenges
Low Latency Processing	Rapid execution of trades to capitalize on market movements.	Achieving millisecond-level processing speeds.
High Throughput	Ability to handle large volumes of market data and transactions concurrently.	Managing data overload and ensuring system stability.
Decentralized Decision-Making	Reduced risk of single points of failure and improved resilience.	Coordinating strategies among multiple independent agents.
Predictive Analytics	Enhanced decision-making with forecasting and dynamic adjustments.	Integrating complex ML models without introducing excessive latency.

LangGraph's flexible and scalable architecture enables its application in a variety of high-demand domains. In the realm of autonomous robotics and IoT systems, LangGraph facilitates the design of responsive and adaptive robotic systems capable of real-time sensor monitoring and dynamic behavioral adjustments. In the financial sector, LangGraph supports the creation of algorithmic trading systems that process market data in real time and execute trades based on automated decision-making.

The code examples and case studies presented in this chapter illustrate practical implementations and provide a foundation for building complex, distributed applications using LangGraph. By leveraging these techniques, developers can create systems that are both resilient and agile, meeting the rigorous demands of real-world applications in robotics, IoT, and finance.

12.3 Smart Cities and Infrastructure Management

Smart cities aim to use technology to improve the efficiency and quality of urban services, making cities more sustainable, livable, and resilient. LangGraph offers a robust framework for developing multi-agent systems that support urban planning and resource management through real-time data collection, dynamic decision-making, and adaptive control.

Applications in Urban Planning

Smart cities deploy autonomous agents to manage various urban services, including:

- **Traffic Management:**
  Agents control traffic signals, monitor congestion, and reroute traffic to optimize flow. Real-time adjustments help reduce commute times and lower pollution levels.
- **Public Safety and Emergency Response:**
  Agents coordinate surveillance cameras, emergency services, and public alerts. They can detect incidents (e.g., accidents, fires) and dispatch appropriate responders quickly.
- **Waste Management:**
  Sensors and robotic systems monitor waste levels and optimize collection routes, reducing operational costs and environmental impact.
- **Energy Distribution:**
  Autonomous agents monitor energy usage and dynamically adjust distribution systems to balance load and integrate renewable energy sources.

Applications in Infrastructure Management

Effective infrastructure management in smart cities includes:

- **Predictive Maintenance:**
  Sensors embedded in roads, bridges, and buildings continuously monitor structural integrity. Agents analyze data to predict maintenance needs, reducing downtime and preventing failures.
- **Resource Allocation:**
  Distributed agents manage public resources (e.g., water, electricity) by dynamically allocating supply based on real-time demand, improving efficiency and reducing waste.

- **Urban Environment Monitoring:**
  Air quality, noise levels, and environmental conditions are tracked by sensors. Agents coordinate to provide actionable insights for urban planners.

Benefits and Challenges

Application Area	Benefits	Challenges
Traffic Management	Reduced congestion, lower emissions, improved commute times	Real-time data processing, integration across disparate systems
Public Safety	Faster emergency response, enhanced situational awareness	Ensuring reliable communication under high load
Waste Management	Cost savings, environmental benefits	Coordinating dynamic routing, data accuracy from sensors
Predictive Maintenance	Preventive repairs, increased infrastructure longevity	Handling large volumes of sensor data, false positives

Code Example: Simulating a Traffic Light Control Agent

Below is a simplified Python simulation using LangGraph to model a traffic light control agent that adapts its signal timings based on simulated traffic density.

python

```python
# traffic_light_agent.py

import asyncio
import random
from langgraph import Agent

class TrafficLightAgent(Agent):
    """

    An agent representing a traffic light at an intersection.
    It adjusts signal timings based on simulated traffic density.
```

```python
    """
    def __init__(self, name):
        super().__init__(name)
        self.signal_state = "green"  # Possible states: green, yellow, red

    async def monitor_traffic(self):
        """
        Simulate monitoring of traffic density at the intersection.
        """
        while True:
            # Simulate traffic density as a random value (vehicles per minute)
            traffic_density = random.randint(10, 100)
            print(f"{self.name} detected traffic density: {traffic_density}
vehicles/min")
            self.adjust_signal(traffic_density)
            # Wait for 3 seconds before next measurement
            await asyncio.sleep(3)

    def adjust_signal(self, traffic_density):
        """
        Adjust the traffic light signal based on traffic density.
        """
        if traffic_density > 70:
            self.signal_state = "red"
        elif 40 < traffic_density <= 70:
            self.signal_state = "yellow"
        else:
            self.signal_state = "green"
        print(f"{self.name} changed signal to: {self.signal_state}")

# Example usage:
async def main():
    traffic_agent = TrafficLightAgent("Intersection_1")
    await traffic_agent.monitor_traffic()

if __name__ == "__main__":
    asyncio.run(main())
```

Explanation:

- The TrafficLightAgent class simulates a traffic light using asynchronous monitoring.

- The monitor_traffic() method generates random traffic density values periodically.
- The adjust_signal() method changes the signal state based on predefined thresholds.
- This example demonstrates how agents can adapt in real time to fluctuating urban conditions.

12.4 Healthcare and Personalized Medicine

The healthcare sector is increasingly leveraging technology to provide personalized, patient-centric care. Multi-agent systems built on LangGraph can help manage vast amounts of data, automate monitoring, and support decision-making in clinical settings.

Customizing Multi-Agent Systems for Healthcare Solutions

In healthcare, LangGraph can be applied to several key areas:

- **Patient Monitoring:**
  Autonomous agents can continuously monitor patient vitals through wearable devices and medical sensors, alerting healthcare providers when anomalies occur.
- **Personalized Treatment Plans:**
  Agents analyze patient data, including medical history, genetic information, and real-time vitals, to recommend tailored treatment regimens.
- **Hospital Resource Management:**
  Multi-agent systems can optimize the allocation of critical resources such as ICU beds, medical staff, and equipment, ensuring that patients receive timely care.
- **Remote Telemedicine:**
  Agents facilitate virtual consultations by managing scheduling, data exchange, and even preliminary diagnostic assessments.

Benefits and Challenges

Healthcare Domain	Benefits	Challenges
Patient Monitoring	Real-time alerts, improved patient outcomes	Data privacy, integration with diverse medical devices
Personalized Treatment	Tailored care, better treatment efficacy	Complex data analysis, regulatory compliance
Resource Management	Efficient use of hospital resources, reduced wait times	Dynamic scheduling, real-time data processing
Telemedicine	Increased access to care, reduced travel for patients	Ensuring secure communication, managing high volumes of data

Code Example: Simulating a Healthcare Monitoring Agent

Below is an example of a healthcare monitoring agent that simulates the continuous monitoring of a patient's heart rate. The agent adjusts its alert level based on the readings.

python

```python
# healthcare_agent.py

import asyncio
import random
from langgraph import Agent

class HealthcareAgent(Agent):
    """
    An agent that monitors a patient's heart rate and triggers alerts when
    abnormal values are detected.
    """
    def __init__(self, name):
        super().__init__(name)
        self.alert_level = "normal"  # Possible levels: normal, caution, critical

    async def monitor_heart_rate(self):
        """
        Asynchronously monitor the patient's heart rate.
```

```python
    """
    while True:
        # Simulate heart rate readings (in beats per minute)
        heart_rate = random.randint(50, 130)
        print(f"{self.name} measured heart rate: {heart_rate} BPM")
        self.evaluate_heart_rate(heart_rate)
        # Wait for 2 seconds before the next reading
        await asyncio.sleep(2)

def evaluate_heart_rate(self, heart_rate):
    """
    Adjust alert level based on the heart rate reading.
    """
    if heart_rate < 60 or heart_rate > 110:
        self.alert_level = "critical"
    elif 60 <= heart_rate <= 70 or 100 <= heart_rate <= 110:
        self.alert_level = "caution"
    else:
        self.alert_level = "normal"
    print(f"{self.name} set alert level to: {self.alert_level}")

# Example usage:
async def main():
    healthcare_agent = HealthcareAgent("Patient_Monitor_1")
    await healthcare_agent.monitor_heart_rate()

if __name__ == "__main__":
    asyncio.run(main())
```

Explanation:

- The HealthcareAgent class simulates patient monitoring by periodically generating random heart rate values.
- The monitor_heart_rate() method uses asynchronous execution to simulate continuous monitoring without blocking.
- The evaluate_heart_rate() method sets the alert level based on the simulated heart rate, mimicking how agents could alert medical staff when a patient's condition deviates from the norm.
- This example demonstrates the potential for multi-agent systems in personalized medicine and remote patient monitoring.

Customization and Integration Considerations

- **Data Security and Privacy:**
  In healthcare applications, it is crucial to ensure that patient data is encrypted and handled in compliance with regulatory standards such as HIPAA or GDPR.
- **Interoperability:**
  Agents must be designed to integrate seamlessly with various medical devices and electronic health records (EHR) systems, often requiring standardized communication protocols.
- **Adaptive Decision-Making:**
  Incorporating machine learning models can help agents continuously improve their predictive accuracy and personalize treatment recommendations.

Summary Table: Healthcare Applications of LangGraph

Application Area	Description	Benefits	Challenges
Patient Monitoring	Continuous monitoring of vital signs and health metrics.	Timely alerts, improved patient outcomes	Data privacy, real-time integration with medical devices
Personalized Treatment	Customizing treatment plans based on patient data analytics.	Tailored therapies, increased treatment efficacy	Complex data processing, compliance with regulations
Resource Management	Optimizing allocation of hospital resources and staff.	Reduced wait times, efficient use of resources	Dynamic scheduling, real-time coordination
Telemedicine	Enabling remote patient consultations and preliminary diagnostics.	Increased accessibility, reduced patient travel costs	Ensuring secure communication, managing high data volumes

LangGraph provides a versatile and powerful framework for building multi-agent systems that can be applied in diverse domains. In the context of smart cities and infrastructure management, LangGraph enables the design of responsive urban systems that optimize traffic, resource allocation, and infrastructure maintenance. In healthcare, LangGraph facilitates the development of personalized monitoring and treatment solutions that improve patient outcomes and optimize hospital operations.

Through practical code examples and detailed use case discussions, this chapter has illustrated how LangGraph can be customized and integrated to address real-world challenges. By leveraging these techniques, developers can create scalable, adaptive, and efficient systems that drive innovation in urban planning and personalized medicine.

12.5 Industry Case Studies and Success Stories

In this section, we explore detailed walkthroughs of successful implementations of LangGraph in various industries. These case studies illustrate how multi-agent systems built with LangGraph have been deployed to solve complex, real-world challenges, improve operational efficiency, and drive innovation. We will discuss examples from smart cities, industrial IoT, financial services, and healthcare. Each case study highlights the system architecture, key performance metrics, challenges addressed, and lessons learned.

Case Study 1: Smart City Traffic Management System

Overview

A major metropolitan city implemented a traffic management system using LangGraph to coordinate thousands of autonomous agents representing traffic signals, environmental sensors, and surveillance cameras. The objective was to optimize traffic flow, reduce congestion, and improve emergency response times.

Implementation Details

- **Architecture:**
  A hybrid architecture was adopted. A central control module was responsible for high-level policy decisions (e.g., adjusting signal

timings based on city-wide traffic patterns), while local clusters of traffic signals operated autonomously at intersections.
- **Technologies Used:**
  - o **LangGraph Framework:** Managed agent creation, inter-agent communication, and dynamic network updates.
  - o **Cloud Infrastructure:** Deployed on AWS using EC2 for compute and S3 for data storage.
  - o **Kubernetes:** Orchestrated containerized LangGraph agents for scalability and high availability.
  - o **Real-Time Analytics:** Integrated with Prometheus and Grafana to monitor traffic data and system performance.

Key Performance Metrics

- **Average Reduction in Congestion:** 25% improvement in traffic flow during peak hours.
- **Response Time:** Average signal adjustment latency was reduced to under 200 milliseconds.
- **System Uptime:** Achieved 99.9% uptime through distributed clustering and redundancy.

Lessons Learned

- **Decentralization is Critical:** Partitioning the network into local clusters reduced the load on the central controller and minimized network latency.
- **Real-Time Monitoring:** Continuous monitoring enabled proactive adjustments and rapid fault detection.
- **Scalability through Containerization:** Using Docker and Kubernetes allowed the system to scale dynamically as traffic patterns changed.

Summary Table: Smart City Traffic Management

Aspect	Details
Architecture	Hybrid (centralized policy + decentralized local control)
Key Technologies	LangGraph, AWS EC2/S3, Kubernetes, Prometheus, Grafana

Aspect	Details
Performance Metrics	25% congestion reduction; <200ms signal latency; 99.9% uptime
Lessons Learned	Importance of decentralization, real-time monitoring, and containerization

Case Study 2: Industrial IoT for Predictive Maintenance

Overview

A large manufacturing plant deployed a multi-agent system using LangGraph to monitor machinery and predict maintenance needs. The goal was to minimize unplanned downtime, reduce maintenance costs, and extend the life of equipment.

Implementation Details

- **Architecture:**
  The system used a modular, decentralized architecture. Each production unit had its own set of sensors and control agents, which communicated with a central monitoring hub for predictive analysis.
- **Technologies Used:**
  - **LangGraph Framework:** Coordinated sensor data collection and agent communication.
  - **Edge Computing:** Deployed agents on local controllers to process data near the source.
  - **Machine Learning Models:** Integrated pre-trained models for anomaly detection and maintenance prediction.
  - **Cloud Storage:** Used for long-term data storage and historical trend analysis.

Key Performance Metrics

- **Downtime Reduction:** Reduced unplanned downtime by 30%.
- **Maintenance Cost Savings:** Achieved 20% cost savings through timely maintenance.
- **Prediction Accuracy:** Machine learning models attained an accuracy rate of 92% in predicting equipment failures.

Lessons Learned

- **Local Processing is Essential:** Edge computing reduces latency and improves response time in critical operations.
- **Data-Driven Decisions:** Integration of ML models enhances predictive maintenance capabilities.
- **Modular Design:** Independent modules for each production unit enable targeted scalability and resilience.

Summary Table: Industrial IoT for Predictive Maintenance

Aspect	Details
Architecture	Decentralized with edge computing and central monitoring
Key Technologies	LangGraph, Edge Devices, ML Models, Cloud Storage
Performance Metrics	30% downtime reduction; 20% maintenance cost savings; 92% prediction accuracy
Lessons Learned	Importance of local processing, data-driven maintenance, and modularity

---

Case Study 3: Financial Algorithmic Trading System

Overview

A financial services firm implemented a distributed algorithmic trading system using LangGraph to manage high-frequency trading operations. The system coordinated hundreds of trading agents that executed real-time trades based on market data and predictive analytics.

Implementation Details

- **Architecture:**
  A decentralized architecture was employed to minimize latency. Each trading agent operated independently, processing market data locally while sharing critical information with a central risk management module.
- **Technologies Used:**
  - **LangGraph Framework:** Provided a robust platform for coordinating multiple trading agents.
  - **Low-Latency Networks:** Utilized dedicated network channels to achieve sub-millisecond communication delays.

- Predictive Analytics: Integrated machine learning models to forecast market trends and adjust trading strategies.
- Cloud Deployment: Deployed on Google Cloud Platform (GCP) to leverage global data centers for reduced latency.

Key Performance Metrics

- **Latency:** Trade execution latency was maintained at under 2 milliseconds.
- **Throughput:** The system processed over 10,000 trades per second.
- **System Resilience:** The decentralized approach ensured continuous operation even during market volatility.

Lessons Learned

- **Ultra-Low Latency is Crucial:** Decentralized decision-making and dedicated networks are essential for high-frequency trading.
- **Integration of AI:** Machine learning models significantly improved predictive accuracy and trading performance.
- **Robust Monitoring:** Continuous real-time monitoring enabled rapid adjustments and minimized risks.

Summary Table: Financial Algorithmic Trading System

Aspect	Details
Architecture	Decentralized with central risk management
Key Technologies	LangGraph, Low-Latency Networks, ML Models, GCP
Performance Metrics	<2ms latency; 10,000+ trades per second; high resilience
Lessons Learned	Critical need for low latency, effective AI integration, and robust monitoring

Case Study 4: Healthcare Monitoring and Personalized Medicine

Overview

A healthcare provider implemented a multi-agent system using LangGraph to monitor patient vitals in real time and provide personalized treatment recommendations. The system integrated data from wearable devices, electronic health records (EHR), and medical imaging to deliver timely interventions.

Implementation Details

- **Architecture:**
  The system featured a hybrid architecture with both centralized data aggregation and decentralized patient monitoring. Each patient's data was processed locally by dedicated agents, which then communicated with a central analysis module.
- **Technologies Used:**
  - **LangGraph Framework:** Managed the coordination between wearable devices, monitoring agents, and central systems.
  - **Cloud and Edge Computing:** Combined to process data close to the patient while storing historical records in the cloud.
  - **AI and Predictive Analytics:** Deployed for early detection of critical conditions and personalized treatment planning.
  - **Secure Communication:** Ensured compliance with HIPAA and GDPR regulations through robust encryption and access controls.

Key Performance Metrics

- **Alert Response Time:** Reduced average response time to critical alerts to under 30 seconds.
- **Patient Outcome Improvement:** Notable improvements in patient outcomes, with a 15% reduction in emergency hospitalizations.
- **Data Accuracy:** Achieved over 95% accuracy in predictive models for patient health deterioration.

Lessons Learned

- **Data Security is Paramount:** Ensuring compliance with healthcare regulations is essential for patient trust.
- **Real-Time and Predictive Analytics:** Combining real-time monitoring with AI-driven predictions leads to better patient outcomes.
- **Scalable and Adaptive Systems:** A hybrid architecture allows for localized processing while maintaining centralized oversight.

Summary Table: Healthcare Monitoring and Personalized Medicine

Aspect	Details
Architecture	Hybrid: decentralized patient monitoring with centralized analysis
Key Technologies	LangGraph, Edge and Cloud Computing, AI Models, Secure Communication
Performance Metrics	<30s alert response; 15% reduction in emergency hospitalizations; 95%+ prediction accuracy
Lessons Learned	Emphasis on data security, real-time analytics, and scalable architectures

The industry case studies presented in this section showcase the versatility and effectiveness of LangGraph in real-world applications. From smart city traffic management to industrial IoT predictive maintenance, high-frequency financial trading, and healthcare monitoring, LangGraph has proven to be a robust framework for building distributed, scalable, and adaptive multi-agent systems.

Key Success Factors:

- **Decentralized and Hybrid Architectures:**
  These architectures ensure resilience, reduce latency, and allow systems to scale dynamically.
- **Integration of Advanced Analytics:**
  Machine learning and predictive analytics enhance decision-making, leading to significant performance improvements.
- **Continuous Monitoring and Real-Time Adjustments:**
  Effective monitoring systems enable rapid responses to changing conditions, ensuring optimal system performance and reliability.
- **Compliance and Security:**
  Particularly in sensitive domains such as healthcare, ensuring data protection and regulatory adherence is crucial.

By learning from these success stories and implementing the best practices outlined, organizations can harness the power of LangGraph to drive innovation, optimize operations, and achieve superior outcomes in a variety of industries.

Chapter 13: Troubleshooting and Maintenance

Ensuring the long-term reliability and performance of your LangGraph-based multi-agent system involves ongoing troubleshooting and maintenance. This chapter covers common pitfalls and design flaws that can undermine system stability, as well as advanced debugging techniques and tools to help you isolate and resolve problems efficiently.

13.1 Common Pitfalls and How to Avoid Them

When developing and maintaining multi-agent systems, various challenges and errors may arise. Identifying and addressing these common pitfalls early can save time and reduce downtime.

Typical Errors and Design Flaws

1. **Inefficient Communication Patterns**
   - **Pitfall:**
     Overuse of broadcast messaging or poorly designed message routing can lead to communication bottlenecks and increased latency.
   - **Avoidance Strategies:**
     - **Implement Targeted Messaging:**
       Design agents to subscribe only to relevant events.
     - **Optimize Message Serialization:**
       Use lightweight serialization formats (e.g., MessagePack) to reduce payload size.
2. **Improper Handling of Asynchronous Operations**
   - **Pitfall:**
     Blocking operations within asynchronous workflows can stall the entire system, causing delays and unresponsive behavior.
   - **Avoidance Strategies:**
     - **Use Asynchronous Libraries Correctly:**
       Leverage Python's asyncio properly by using await on I/O-bound tasks.

- **Avoid Synchronous Calls in Async Functions:**
  Ensure that long-running computations are offloaded or optimized.

3. **Resource Leaks and Memory Management Issues**
   - **Pitfall:**
     Failure to release resources (e.g., file handles, network sockets) and improper memory management can lead to degraded performance and crashes.
   - **Avoidance Strategies:**
     - **Use Context Managers:**
       Implement with statements for file operations and network connections.
     - **Monitor Resource Usage:**
       Utilize profiling tools to track memory usage and detect leaks.

4. **Inadequate Error Handling and Logging**
   - **Pitfall:**
     Unhandled exceptions or lack of detailed logging makes it difficult to diagnose issues in a distributed system.
   - **Avoidance Strategies:**
     - **Implement Comprehensive Error Handling:**
       Use try-except blocks to capture exceptions and implement fallback procedures.
     - **Adopt Structured Logging:**
       Log errors in a structured format (e.g., JSON) for easy parsing and analysis.

5. **Poor Scalability Due to Centralized Bottlenecks**
   - **Pitfall:**
     Relying on a single coordinator or central node for decision-making can create a single point of failure and limit scalability.
   - **Avoidance Strategies:**
     - **Decentralize Control:**
       Distribute responsibilities among agents to reduce the load on any one component.
     - **Implement Redundancy and Load Balancing:**
       Use auto-scaling and load balancers to distribute workload evenly.

Summary Table: Common Pitfalls and Mitigation Strategies

Pitfall	Description	Mitigation Strategy
Inefficient Communication	Excessive broadcasts, unoptimized routing	Targeted messaging, lightweight serialization formats
Blocking Asynchronous Operations	Synchronous calls in async functions causing delays	Proper use of asyncio, offload heavy computations
Resource Leaks	Unreleased file handles, network sockets, and memory not freed	Use context managers, monitor resource usage with profilers
Inadequate Error Handling	Unhandled exceptions and poor logging hinder troubleshooting	Comprehensive try-except blocks, structured logging
Centralized Bottlenecks	Single point of failure that limits scalability	Decentralized architectures, redundancy, load balancing

13.2 Advanced Debugging Techniques and Tools

Efficient troubleshooting in a multi-agent system requires advanced debugging techniques and specialized tools that allow you to isolate and resolve problems quickly.

Strategies for Effective Problem Isolation

1. **Comprehensive Logging and Auditing**
   - **Technique:**
     Use structured logging to capture detailed information about agent activities, errors, and system events.
   - **Best Practices:**
     - **Centralized Logging Systems:**
       Aggregate logs using tools like the ELK Stack (Elasticsearch, Logstash, Kibana) or Splunk.
     - **Log Levels:**
       Use different log levels (DEBUG, INFO, WARNING,

ERROR, CRITICAL) to control the verbosity and focus on critical issues during troubleshooting.

2. **Distributed Tracing**
   - **Technique:**
   Track the flow of requests across multiple agents to pinpoint latency issues or failures.
   - **Tools:**
     - **Jaeger and Zipkin:**
     Implement distributed tracing to visualize interactions and identify bottlenecks.

3. **Profiling and Performance Monitoring**
   - **Technique:**
   Use profiling tools to measure execution times, memory usage, and identify performance hotspots.
   - **Tools:**
     - **cProfile, Py-Spy, and Line Profiler:**
     Provide detailed insights into function calls and execution times.
     - **System Monitoring Tools:**
     Tools like Prometheus and Grafana can help monitor real-time system performance.

4. **Interactive Debugging**
   - **Technique:**
   Use interactive debuggers to inspect and modify the state of a running system.
   - **Tools:**
     - **pdb (Python Debugger):**
     Allows you to step through code execution, inspect variables, and evaluate expressions.
     - **Integrated Development Environment (IDE) Debuggers:**
     IDEs like PyCharm or VSCode offer advanced debugging features that simplify problem isolation.

Example: Using pdb for Interactive Debugging

Below is an example of how to use Python's built-in pdb module to debug a simple function within an agent.

python

debug_example.py

```
def faulty_function(x):
    result = x * 2
    # Introduce an error for demonstration purposes
    faulty_result = result / 0  # This will raise a ZeroDivisionError
    return faulty_result

if __name__ == "__main__":
    import pdb
    pdb.set_trace()  # Set a breakpoint here
    value = 10
    print("Starting calculation...")
    try:
        output = faulty_function(value)
    except ZeroDivisionError as e:
        print(f"Error encountered: {e}")
    print("Calculation complete.")
```

Explanation:

- **pdb.set_trace():**
  This line sets a breakpoint that pauses execution, allowing you to interactively inspect the program's state.
- **Faulty Function:**
  The function intentionally introduces a ZeroDivisionError to demonstrate how you can trace the error.
- **Error Handling:**
  The try-except block catches the error and prints an informative message, making it easier to isolate and understand the problem.

Summary Table: Advanced Debugging Techniques and Tools

Technique	Tool/Method	Description	Benefits
Comprehensive Logging	ELK Stack, Splunk, Python logging module	Captures detailed system events and errors in a structured format	Facilitates quick diagnosis and historical analysis
Distributed Tracing	Jaeger, Zipkin	Visualizes the flow of requests across distributed systems	Identifies bottlenecks and inter-agent

Technique	Tool/Method	Description	Benefits
			communication issues
Profiling	cProfile, Py-Spy, Line Profiler	Measures execution time and resource usage	Pinpoints performance hotspots and optimization areas
Interactive Debugging	pdb, IDE debuggers (PyCharm, VSCode)	Allows step-by-step code execution and state inspection	Accelerates troubleshooting and reduces downtime

Troubleshooting and maintenance are critical components of managing a robust multi-agent system built with LangGraph. By understanding common pitfalls—such as inefficient communication, blocking asynchronous operations, resource leaks, inadequate error handling, and centralized bottlenecks—you can proactively design solutions to avoid them. Moreover, employing advanced debugging techniques, including comprehensive logging, distributed tracing, profiling, and interactive debugging, enables you to isolate and resolve issues effectively.

The strategies and tools discussed in this chapter provide a structured approach to diagnosing and addressing problems, ensuring that your LangGraph-based system remains reliable, efficient, and scalable. Regular maintenance, coupled with a proactive debugging strategy, forms the backbone of a well-managed distributed system, enabling continuous improvement and operational excellence.

13.3 Maintaining and Updating Your System

Continuous maintenance and periodic updates are essential for ensuring that your multi-agent system remains secure, efficient, and capable of evolving with new requirements. This section outlines best practices for continuous improvement, proactive system monitoring, and regular updates.

Best Practices for Continuous Improvement

1. **Regular System Audits and Reviews**
   - **Periodic Code Reviews:**
     Conduct regular code reviews to ensure that the system

adheres to best practices, coding standards, and design principles.
- o **Performance Audits:**
  Regularly profile and benchmark the system to identify performance bottlenecks or resource leaks that might degrade system performance over time.
- o **Security Audits:**
  Perform vulnerability assessments and penetration testing to identify and remediate security flaws.

2. **Automated Monitoring and Alerting**
   - o **Real-Time Monitoring:**
     Utilize tools such as Prometheus and Grafana to monitor system performance metrics (CPU, memory, network latency, etc.) continuously.
   - o **Alert Systems:**
     Set up automated alerts for unusual behavior, such as spikes in error rates or resource usage, to facilitate prompt responses.

3. **Scheduled Updates and Maintenance Windows**
   - o **Rolling Updates:**
     Implement rolling updates to deploy new versions of agents or modules gradually, minimizing downtime and allowing for quick rollback if issues are detected.
   - o **Maintenance Windows:**
     Plan regular maintenance periods during low-usage times to apply patches, update libraries, and perform database backups.

4. **Documentation and Knowledge Sharing**
   - o **Comprehensive Documentation:**
     Maintain up-to-date documentation on system architecture, configuration, and troubleshooting procedures.
   - o **Change Logs and Release Notes:**
     Keep detailed records of changes, updates, and improvements made to the system for future reference and compliance purposes.

5. **Feedback Loops and Continuous Integration**
   - o **User Feedback:**
     Incorporate feedback from system users and administrators to drive improvements and address emerging needs.
   - o **Continuous Integration (CI):**
     Integrate automated testing and CI pipelines to ensure that updates do not introduce new issues.

Example: Automated Maintenance Check Script

Below is a simple Python script that demonstrates an automated maintenance check. This script could be scheduled (using cron or a similar tool) to run at regular intervals and report on key system metrics.

python

```python
# maintenance_check.py

import psutil
import logging
from datetime import datetime

# Configure logging to a maintenance log file
logging.basicConfig(filename='maintenance.log', level=logging.INFO,
            format='%(asctime)s - %(levelname)s - %(message)s')

def check_cpu_usage(threshold=80):
    """Check the current CPU usage and log a warning if it exceeds the
threshold."""
    cpu_usage = psutil.cpu_percent(interval=1)
    if cpu_usage > threshold:
        logging.warning(f"High CPU usage detected: {cpu_usage}%")
    else:
        logging.info(f"CPU usage is normal: {cpu_usage}%")
    return cpu_usage

def check_memory_usage(threshold=80):
    """Check the current memory usage and log a warning if it exceeds the
threshold."""
    memory = psutil.virtual_memory()
    mem_usage = memory.percent
    if mem_usage > threshold:
        logging.warning(f"High memory usage detected: {mem_usage}%")
    else:
        logging.info(f"Memory usage is normal: {mem_usage}%")
    return mem_usage

def perform_maintenance_check():
    """Perform a series of maintenance checks and log the results."""
    logging.info("Starting maintenance check.")
```

```
check_cpu_usage()
check_memory_usage()
logging.info("Maintenance check completed.")

if __name__ == "__main__":
    perform_maintenance_check()
```

Explanation:

- **psutil Library:**
  The script uses the psutil library to monitor system metrics such as CPU and memory usage.
- **Logging:**
  It logs important events (e.g., high resource usage) to a file named maintenance.log.
- **Automated Check:**
  This script can be run periodically to ensure the system is operating within acceptable parameters.

Summary Table: Maintenance Best Practices

Practice	Description	Benefits
Regular Code and Performance Audits	Periodic reviews and profiling of code and system performance	Early detection of issues; continuous improvement
Automated Monitoring and Alerts	Use of real-time tools and automated notifications	Prompt response to anomalies; proactive maintenance
Scheduled Updates and Maintenance Windows	Planned update intervals and rolling deployments	Minimal downtime; safe, gradual updates
Comprehensive Documentation	Detailed records of system changes and operational procedures	Easier troubleshooting; knowledge sharing among teams
Continuous Integration	Automated testing and integration pipelines	Ensures stability and prevents regressions

13.4 Disaster Recovery and Failover Strategies

Despite the best preventive measures, unexpected downtime and failures can occur. Disaster recovery and failover strategies are essential for ensuring that your system can quickly recover from failures and continue operating with minimal disruption.

Key Components of Disaster Recovery Planning

1. **Data Backup and Restoration**
   - **Regular Backups:**
     Schedule regular backups of critical data (e.g., databases, configuration files) to secure, off-site storage.
   - **Restoration Testing:**
     Regularly test backup restoration processes to ensure data can be recovered quickly in the event of a failure.
2. **Redundancy and Failover Mechanisms**
   - **Active-Passive Failover:**
     Maintain standby systems that automatically take over if the primary system fails.
   - **Active-Active Configuration:**
     Deploy multiple active systems that share the workload, ensuring continuous operation even if one system encounters an issue.
   - **Health Checks and Heartbeats:**
     Implement regular health checks for system components. Use heartbeat signals to monitor the status of critical services.
3. **Disaster Recovery Plan (DRP)**
   - **DRP Documentation:**
     Develop and maintain a comprehensive disaster recovery plan outlining procedures, responsibilities, and contact information.
   - **Regular DRP Drills:**
     Conduct drills and simulations to test the effectiveness of your disaster recovery plan, and update it based on lessons learned.

Example: Simple Failover Simulation Script

Below is a Python script that simulates a failover scenario. This script demonstrates how an agent might detect a failure and trigger a backup process.

python

```python
# failover_simulation.py

import time
import random

def check_system_health():
    """Simulate a system health check that randomly fails."""
    # Randomly return False to simulate a system failure
    return random.choice([True, True, True, False])

def trigger_failover():
    """Simulate triggering a failover process."""
    print("System failure detected! Initiating failover...")
    # Simulate time taken for failover
    time.sleep(2)
    print("Failover complete. Backup system is now active.")

def monitor_system():
    """Monitor the system health and trigger failover if necessary."""
    while True:
        health = check_system_health()
        if not health:
            trigger_failover()
        else:
            print("System is healthy.")
        # Wait for 5 seconds before the next health check
        time.sleep(5)

if __name__ == "__main__":
    monitor_system()
```

Explanation:

- **Health Check Simulation:**
  The check_system_health() function simulates a health check that randomly fails, representing an unexpected system outage.
- **Failover Process:**
  The trigger_failover() function simulates a failover process, pausing for a short duration to represent the time taken to switch to a backup system.

- **Continuous Monitoring:**
  The monitor_system() function continuously checks system health and triggers the failover process when a failure is detected.

Summary Table: Disaster Recovery and Failover Strategies

Component	Technique	Benefits	Example
Data Backup	Regular, automated backups to off-site storage	Ensures data is preserved and can be restored after a failure	Scheduled backup scripts
Failover Mechanisms	Active-Passive and Active-Active configurations	Minimizes downtime; provides redundancy	Automated failover scripts; load balancers
Health Monitoring	Regular health checks and heartbeat signals	Early detection of failures; proactive recovery	Scripts that simulate system health and trigger failover
Disaster Recovery Plan (DRP)	Documented procedures and regular drills	Provides clear guidelines for rapid recovery; ensures readiness	DRP documentation and periodic drills

Maintaining and updating your LangGraph-based system, as well as planning for disaster recovery, are critical aspects of ensuring long-term operational excellence. In this section, we discussed best practices for continuous maintenance, including regular audits, automated monitoring, scheduled updates, and thorough documentation. These practices enable continuous improvement and help prevent common pitfalls that can degrade system performance.

We also explored disaster recovery and failover strategies, highlighting the importance of data backup, redundancy, and regular testing of recovery procedures. The provided examples and summary tables offer practical guidance on implementing these strategies, ensuring that your system can recover quickly from unexpected downtimes and continue operating smoothly.

By following these best practices and planning meticulously for both routine maintenance and disaster recovery, you can enhance the reliability, resilience, and longevity of your multi-agent system built on LangGraph.

13.5 Performance Tuning and Ongoing Monitoring

Keeping Your System Healthy Over Time

Maintaining optimal performance and ensuring system health is an ongoing process, especially in complex, distributed multi-agent systems built with LangGraph. Performance tuning and continuous monitoring are key components of this process, as they help detect issues before they escalate, optimize resource usage, and guarantee that the system operates at peak efficiency over time. In this section, we detail best practices, methodologies, and tools for performance tuning and ongoing monitoring.

Key Areas of Focus

1. **Performance Tuning:**
   Performance tuning involves identifying bottlenecks and optimizing various aspects of your system to improve efficiency and responsiveness. This can include optimizing code execution, reducing latency in communication between agents, and fine-tuning resource allocation.
2. **Ongoing Monitoring:**
   Continuous monitoring ensures that system health is maintained by tracking key performance metrics such as CPU usage, memory consumption, network latency, and error rates. This enables proactive identification of issues and rapid response to anomalies.

Performance Tuning Strategies

1. Code Optimization

- **Profiling:**
  Use profiling tools (e.g., cProfile, Py-Spy, Line Profiler) to analyze your code and identify functions or methods that are consuming excessive CPU time or memory.

Example:
Running cProfile on a critical function:

python

```python
import cProfile, pstats

def heavy_computation():
    total = 0
    for i in range(1, 1000000):
        total += i ** 0.5
    return total

if __name__ == "__main__":
    profiler = cProfile.Profile()
    profiler.enable()
    result = heavy_computation()
    profiler.disable()
    print(f"Result: {result}")
    stats = pstats.Stats(profiler).sort_stats('cumulative')
    stats.print_stats(10)
```

Explanation:
This code profiles the heavy_computation() function to identify how much time is spent in each part of the computation, allowing targeted optimization.

- **Algorithm Optimization:**
  Review and optimize algorithms used within agents. For example, replacing an inefficient search algorithm with a more efficient one can reduce latency.
- **Efficient Data Structures:**
  Use appropriate data structures (e.g., sets for membership testing, tuples for immutable collections) to minimize memory overhead and increase processing speed.

2. Optimizing Agent Interactions and Communication

- **Batching and Aggregation:**
  Instead of processing a large number of small messages individually, batch them together. This reduces communication overhead and minimizes the number of network calls.

- **Asynchronous Processing:**
Leverage asynchronous programming (e.g., Python's asyncio) to allow agents to handle I/O-bound operations concurrently. This prevents blocking and ensures that multiple operations can proceed simultaneously.

Example: Asynchronous Message Processing

python

```python
import asyncio

async def process_message(message):
    # Simulate asynchronous processing
    await asyncio.sleep(0.1)
    print(f"Processed message: {message}")

async def main():
    messages = [f"Message {i}" for i in range(1, 6)]
    # Process messages concurrently
    await asyncio.gather(*(process_message(msg) for msg in messages))

if __name__ == "__main__":
    asyncio.run(main())
```

Explanation:
The example shows how asynchronous processing can handle multiple messages concurrently, reducing wait times compared to sequential processing.

3. Resource Allocation and Load Balancing

- **Dynamic Scaling:**
Use container orchestration platforms like Kubernetes to implement auto-scaling based on real-time resource usage metrics. Adjust the number of agent replicas dynamically to meet demand.
- **Load Balancing:**
Implement load balancing strategies, such as round-robin or weighted distribution, to evenly distribute tasks across agents and prevent any single agent from becoming a bottleneck.

Ongoing Monitoring Best Practices

1. Real-Time Monitoring Tools

- **Prometheus and Grafana:**
  Prometheus collects and stores metrics from various system components, while Grafana visualizes these metrics in real time. Together, they provide a comprehensive monitoring solution.
- **ELK Stack (Elasticsearch, Logstash, Kibana):**
  This suite of tools can aggregate logs, process and index them, and provide powerful visualization and search capabilities to monitor system events and errors.

2. Metrics to Monitor

- **Resource Utilization:**
  Monitor CPU usage, memory consumption, disk I/O, and network bandwidth. High resource utilization may indicate bottlenecks or inefficient processes.
- **Response Times:**
  Track the latency of agent interactions and message processing to ensure that the system is responsive.
- **Error Rates:**
  Monitor logs for exceptions and error messages to quickly identify and resolve issues.
- **Throughput:**
  Measure the number of tasks processed per unit time to ensure that the system can handle the expected load.

3. Setting Up Alerts and Automated Responses

- **Threshold-Based Alerts:**
  Configure alerts to notify administrators when metrics exceed predefined thresholds (e.g., CPU usage > 80%, response time > 200 ms).
- **Automated Recovery:**
  Integrate monitoring tools with automation scripts that can trigger failover processes or restart services when anomalies are detected.

Example: Monitoring with Prometheus and Grafana

Prometheus Configuration Example

A basic Prometheus configuration file (prometheus.yml) might look like this:

yaml

```
global:
  scrape_interval: 15s

scrape_configs:
  - job_name: 'langgraph'
    static_configs:
      - targets: ['localhost:9090', 'localhost:9100']
```

Explanation:

- **Scrape Interval:**
  Prometheus collects metrics every 15 seconds.
- **Job Configuration:**
  A job named langgraph is defined with targets where metrics are available.

Grafana Dashboard

- **Setting Up a Dashboard:**
  In Grafana, create a new dashboard and add panels that display metrics such as CPU usage, memory consumption, and agent response times. Grafana connects to Prometheus as a data source.
- **Visualization:**
  Use line graphs, bar charts, and heatmaps to visualize trends over time. This helps in identifying performance degradation and potential issues.

Summary Table: Performance Tuning and Ongoing Monitoring

Aspect	Techniques/Tools	Benefits	Example
Code Optimization	Profiling (cProfile, Py-Spy), efficient algorithms, data structures	Identify bottlenecks; improve execution speed	cProfile example above
Agent Interaction Optimization	Batching, asynchronous processing (asyncio)	Reduces latency and communication overhead	Async message processing example
Resource Allocation	Dynamic scaling, load balancing	Efficiently distributes workload; prevents bottlenecks	Kubernetes auto-scaling, round-robin scheduler
Monitoring Tools	Prometheus, Grafana, ELK Stack	Real-time performance tracking; prompt anomaly detection	Prometheus configuration example
Alerting & Automated Responses	Threshold alerts, automated recovery scripts	Rapid response to issues; minimized downtime	Automated maintenance scripts

Performance tuning and ongoing monitoring are critical for keeping your LangGraph-based multi-agent system healthy over time. By continuously profiling and optimizing your code, refining communication protocols, and managing resources effectively, you can ensure that your system remains responsive, scalable, and efficient.

Implementing robust monitoring solutions using tools like Prometheus and Grafana, combined with automated alerting and recovery mechanisms, helps in quickly identifying and resolving issues before they impact system performance. The strategies and examples provided in this section serve as a practical guide to achieving continuous performance improvements and maintaining the overall health of your distributed system.

By adopting these best practices, you lay a strong foundation for a resilient, high-performing system capable of adapting to changing loads and evolving requirements, ensuring long-term operational excellence.

Chapter 14: Future Trends and Innovations

The field of autonomous systems is evolving at an unprecedented pace, driven by rapid advancements in artificial intelligence (AI), machine learning (ML), the Internet of Things (IoT), and other emerging technologies. In this chapter, we explore the cutting-edge trends that are shaping the future of autonomous multi-agent systems, and we outline a roadmap for the continued development of LangGraph, highlighting planned features, community contributions, and visionary directions for the framework.

14.1 Emerging Technologies in Autonomous Systems

Emerging technologies are continuously pushing the boundaries of what autonomous systems can achieve. The integration of next-generation AI, ML, and IoT technologies is transforming these systems into smarter, more adaptive, and highly interconnected networks. In this section, we discuss key innovations and trends that are poised to impact the future of autonomous systems.

Next-Generation AI and Machine Learning

- **Deep Learning and Reinforcement Learning:**
  Advanced deep learning models, including deep neural networks and convolutional neural networks (CNNs), are enabling agents to process complex sensory data such as images, audio, and video. Reinforcement learning (RL), and its deep variant (Deep RL), are proving effective for training agents in dynamic environments where they learn optimal behaviors through trial and error. These models empower agents to make decisions in environments with high uncertainty and complexity.
- **Federated Learning:**
  Federated learning allows multiple agents to collaboratively train a shared model while keeping the underlying data local. This is particularly useful for privacy-sensitive applications such as healthcare and finance, where data cannot be centralized. By distributing the learning process, agents can collectively improve their decision-making without compromising data security.

- **Explainable AI (XAI):**
  As AI becomes more complex, the need for transparency and interpretability in decision-making is growing. Explainable AI aims to make the inner workings of AI models more understandable to developers and users alike. This is crucial in domains like autonomous driving and healthcare, where trust in automated decisions is essential.

IoT Integration and Edge Computing

- **Enhanced Sensor Networks:**
  The next generation of IoT devices features improved sensor accuracy, increased connectivity (e.g., 5G networks), and more robust data processing capabilities. These advancements enable agents to receive higher-quality, real-time data, which is critical for making informed decisions.
- **Edge Computing:**
  Edge computing brings data processing closer to the source of data generation, reducing latency and bandwidth usage. By deploying processing capabilities at the network edge, autonomous systems can make faster decisions and operate more reliably, even in environments with intermittent connectivity to centralized data centers.
- **Interoperability and Standardization:**
  The growing ecosystem of IoT devices is driving efforts to standardize communication protocols and data formats. Improved interoperability between heterogeneous devices simplifies the integration process for autonomous systems, enabling seamless collaboration across various platforms and industries.

Other Emerging Trends

- **Blockchain and Decentralized Trust:**
  Blockchain technology is emerging as a powerful tool for enhancing the security and integrity of multi-agent systems. By providing a decentralized and tamper-proof ledger, blockchain can be used to securely record agent interactions, transactions, and decisions, thereby building trust in distributed environments.
- **Quantum Computing:**
  Although still in its early stages, quantum computing promises to revolutionize the processing capabilities of complex systems. Quantum algorithms have the potential to solve optimization and

search problems much faster than classical counterparts, which could significantly enhance decision-making in autonomous systems.

- **Augmented Reality (AR) and Virtual Reality (VR):**
  In applications such as training, simulation, and remote collaboration, AR and VR technologies are enabling immersive experiences that can improve system design and operational efficiency. Agents can be monitored and managed in virtual environments that provide real-time, intuitive feedback on system performance.

Summary Table: Emerging Technologies Impacting Autonomous Systems

Technology	Key Features	Impact on Autonomous Systems
Deep Learning & Reinforcement Learning	Advanced neural networks; trial-and-error learning; high-dimensional data processing	Enhances decision-making; improves adaptability in complex environments
Federated Learning	Collaborative model training; decentralized data; privacy preservation	Enables secure, scalable learning across distributed agents
Explainable AI (XAI)	Transparent decision-making; model interpretability	Builds trust; facilitates debugging and regulatory compliance
Enhanced IoT & Edge Computing	Improved sensor accuracy; reduced latency; localized data processing	Enables real-time responses; reduces network dependency
Blockchain	Decentralized ledger; tamper-proof records	Increases security and trust in agent interactions
Quantum Computing	Exponential processing power; quantum algorithms	Potential for solving complex optimization problems faster
AR/VR Technologies	Immersive visualization; real-time simulation	Enhances training, monitoring, and remote management of systems

14.2 The Future of LangGraph: Roadmap and Vision

As the landscape of autonomous systems evolves, so too must the tools and frameworks that support them. LangGraph is poised to continue its evolution, driven by both planned enhancements and vibrant community contributions. In this section, we outline the future roadmap for LangGraph and articulate a vision that aligns with emerging technologies and industry needs.

Planned Features and Enhancements

1. **Enhanced AI and ML Integration**
   - **Native Support for Federated Learning:**
     Develop modules that facilitate federated learning, allowing agents to collaboratively train models while maintaining data privacy.
   - **Integrated Explainable AI Tools:**
     Incorporate tools and libraries that provide insights into agent decision-making processes, making the system more transparent and trustworthy.
   - **Advanced Reinforcement Learning Frameworks:**
     Build support for deep reinforcement learning, enabling agents to learn from complex, dynamic environments more effectively.
2. **Improved IoT and Edge Computing Capabilities**
   - **Edge Computing Modules:**
     Develop modules that optimize the deployment of LangGraph agents on edge devices, reducing latency and enhancing real-time decision-making.
   - **Interoperability Enhancements:**
     Implement standardized protocols and APIs to seamlessly integrate with a wide range of IoT devices and sensor networks.
3. **Scalability and Performance Optimization**
   - **Auto-Scaling and Dynamic Resource Management:**
     Enhance integration with container orchestration platforms (e.g., Kubernetes) to support automatic scaling based on real-time performance metrics.
   - **Optimized Communication Protocols:**
     Improve the efficiency of inter-agent communication by adopting lightweight serialization formats and advanced load balancing strategies.
4. **Security and Compliance Features**

- o **Enhanced Encryption and Access Control:**
  Integrate more robust security protocols to protect data in transit and at rest, ensuring compliance with industry regulations such as GDPR and HIPAA.
- o **Audit Trails and Compliance Reporting:**
  Develop features that automatically generate audit logs and compliance reports, simplifying regulatory adherence.

5. **Developer and Community Support**
   - o **Comprehensive Documentation and Tutorials:**
     Expand the official documentation, including detailed tutorials, best practices, and troubleshooting guides.
   - o **Community-Driven Modules:**
     Foster an open-source community where developers can contribute custom modules, plugins, and enhancements.
   - o **Regular Release Cycles and Feedback Integration:**
     Establish a predictable release cycle and actively integrate community feedback to prioritize feature development.

Future Vision and Roadmap

The vision for LangGraph is to become the leading framework for building, deploying, and managing scalable, autonomous multi-agent systems across diverse industries. Key elements of this vision include:

- **Interoperability and Flexibility:**
  LangGraph will support seamless integration with emerging technologies, ensuring that it remains adaptable in the rapidly evolving tech landscape.
- **User-Centric Design:**
  Focus on simplifying the development process with intuitive APIs, extensive documentation, and robust community support, enabling both beginners and experts to build sophisticated systems.
- **Cutting-Edge AI and IoT Integration:**
  Leverage the latest advancements in AI, ML, and IoT to provide agents with advanced decision-making capabilities, making autonomous systems smarter and more efficient.
- **Sustainable Scalability and Security:**
  Ensure that LangGraph systems can scale to meet the demands of large, distributed deployments while maintaining high levels of security and regulatory compliance.

Roadmap Table: Future Features for LangGraph

Timeframe	Planned Features	Impact/Benefits
Short Term (0-6 months)	- Improved documentation and tutorials - Integration with basic federated learning modules - Enhanced logging and monitoring features	Accelerates developer onboarding; lays the groundwork for advanced ML integration; improves system observability
Medium Term (6-12 months)	- Auto-scaling and dynamic resource management integration with Kubernetes - Advanced reinforcement learning support - Standardized IoT protocols and edge computing modules	Enhances scalability and performance; enables smarter, data-driven decision-making; ensures seamless IoT integration
Long Term (12-24 months)	- Native support for explainable AI tools - Comprehensive security and compliance features - Broad community-driven module ecosystem	Builds trust through transparency; guarantees regulatory compliance; fosters innovation through community contributions

The future of autonomous systems is being shaped by rapid advances in AI, ML, IoT, and other emerging technologies. LangGraph is well-positioned to harness these innovations and continue evolving as a leading framework for multi-agent systems. By planning for enhanced AI integration, improved scalability and performance, robust security, and vibrant community support, the future roadmap for LangGraph is focused on meeting the demands of an increasingly complex and dynamic technological landscape.

This chapter has provided a detailed exploration of emerging technologies in autonomous systems and outlined a clear vision and roadmap for the future of LangGraph. As developers and organizations adopt these forward-looking strategies, LangGraph will continue to empower the creation of smarter, more adaptive, and highly resilient multi-agent systems that drive innovation across industries.

14.3 Evolving Architectures and Adaptive Systems

As autonomous systems become more complex and the demands on them continue to grow, their underlying architectures must also evolve. Evolving architectures refer to the ways in which system designs are reimagined and adapted over time to meet new challenges, optimize performance, and respond to changing environments. Adaptive systems are those that can automatically adjust their behavior, configurations, or structures in response to internal or external stimuli.

Key Concepts in Evolving Architectures

1. **Modularity and Flexibility:**
   - **Modular Design:**
     Future systems are expected to be built as a collection of interchangeable and independently deployable modules. This design philosophy enables individual components to be updated, replaced, or scaled without impacting the entire system.
   - **Plug-and-Play Capabilities:**
     Systems will allow new modules or services to be integrated with minimal configuration, enabling rapid experimentation and adaptation.
2. **Decentralized and Distributed Control:**
   - **Decentralization:**
     Moving away from centralized control, future architectures will distribute decision-making across multiple agents. This improves fault tolerance, reduces latency, and prevents single points of failure.
   - **Distributed Ledger Technologies:**
     Technologies such as blockchain may be used to maintain integrity and trust in decentralized systems, ensuring that interactions are secure and transparent.
3. **Self-Adaptive and Self-Healing Systems:**
   - **Autonomous Adaptation:**
     Systems will incorporate mechanisms that allow them to monitor their own performance and automatically adjust configurations to optimize resource usage, balance loads, or recover from failures.

- o **Predictive Maintenance:**
  Using machine learning and predictive analytics, systems can anticipate failures or performance degradation and take corrective actions before issues escalate.
4. **Interoperability and Standardization:**
   - o **Standard Protocols:**
     As more heterogeneous devices and agents come online, standardized communication protocols and data formats will be critical for seamless interoperability.
   - o **APIs and Microservices:**
     A move towards microservices architectures will enable systems to interact through well-defined APIs, making it easier to integrate diverse components from various vendors.

Example: Adaptive System Architecture Diagram

Below is a simplified conceptual diagram illustrating an adaptive multi-agent system:

sql

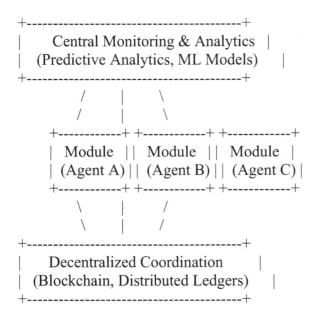

Explanation:

- **Central Monitoring & Analytics:**
  This module gathers data from all agents and applies predictive

analytics and ML models to forecast issues and recommend adjustments.

- **Individual Modules (Agents):**
  Each module represents a component that can operate independently and be updated or scaled as needed.
- **Decentralized Coordination:**
  This layer ensures secure and transparent communication between modules, enabling autonomous decision-making across the system.

Benefits of Evolving Architectures

Aspect	Benefits
Modularity	Easier maintenance and upgrades; flexibility in deployment.
Decentralization	Improved fault tolerance; reduced latency; increased resilience.
Self-Adaptation	Proactive response to performance issues and environmental changes.
Interoperability	Seamless integration with diverse devices and platforms.

14.4 The Role of Open Source and Collaborative Innovation

The future of autonomous systems will be significantly shaped by open source initiatives and collaborative innovation. Open source fosters an environment where knowledge, tools, and innovations are shared, accelerating development and enabling rapid advancement in technology.

Importance of Open Source in Autonomous Systems

1. **Accelerated Development:**
   - **Shared Code and Resources:**
     Open source projects allow developers to build on existing work rather than reinventing the wheel. This accelerates development cycles and fosters innovation.
   - **Community Contributions:**
     A vibrant community of contributors can provide diverse perspectives, identify bugs quickly, and propose improvements that benefit everyone.
2. **Transparency and Trust:**

- o **Open Codebase:**
  An open source codebase allows for peer review and transparency, which helps in building trust among users and stakeholders. This is especially important in critical systems like autonomous vehicles and healthcare.
- o **Security Audits:**
  Community-driven projects often benefit from regular security audits by independent experts, ensuring that vulnerabilities are identified and resolved promptly.

3. **Customization and Flexibility:**
   - o **Tailored Solutions:**
     Organizations can modify open source software to meet their specific needs, adding custom features or integrating with proprietary systems.
   - o **Interoperability:**
     Open source standards and APIs promote interoperability between different systems, facilitating seamless integration across various platforms and technologies.

Collaborative Innovation: Models and Best Practices

1. **Community-Driven Development:**
   - o **GitHub and GitLab:**
     Platforms like GitHub and GitLab serve as hubs for open source projects where developers can contribute code, report issues, and collaborate on new features.
   - o **Contribution Guidelines:**
     Establishing clear contribution guidelines and code standards helps ensure that contributions are high quality and align with the project's vision.
2. **Hackathons and Developer Conferences:**
   - o **Innovation Through Collaboration:**
     Hackathons and developer meetups provide opportunities for real-time collaboration, where developers can experiment with new ideas, create prototypes, and receive immediate feedback.
   - o **Knowledge Sharing:**
     Conferences and webinars allow community members to share their experiences, case studies, and best practices, fostering a culture of continuous learning.
3. **Open Standards and Interoperability Initiatives:**

- **Industry Consortia:**
  Collaboration among industry players through consortia and standardization bodies helps drive the development of open standards, ensuring that technologies remain interoperable and future-proof.

Example: Collaborative Development on GitHub

Below is an example snippet from a GitHub repository README that outlines contribution guidelines for an open source project based on LangGraph:

markdown

LangGraph Open Source Project

Welcome to the LangGraph project! We welcome contributions from developers around the world. Our goal is to build a robust and flexible framework for autonomous multi-agent systems.

How to Contribute

1. **Fork the Repository:**
   - Click the "Fork" button on the top right to create your own copy of the project.

2. **Create a Feature Branch:**
   - Use descriptive names for your branches (e.g., `feature/add-async-support`).

3. **Submit Pull Requests:**
   - Ensure your code follows our coding guidelines and includes tests.
   - Submit a pull request and describe the changes you've made.

4. **Code Reviews:**
   - Our maintainers will review your contributions and provide feedback.
   - Discussions are welcome—our goal is to improve the project together!

Community Resources

- **Discussion Forum:**

Join our community forum to discuss ideas, share use cases, and seek support.
- **Documentation:**
Visit our documentation site for tutorials, API references, and design guidelines.

We appreciate your contributions and look forward to building a better future for autonomous systems together!

Explanation:

- **Contribution Guidelines:**
  Clear steps for how to contribute encourage community participation and maintain code quality.
- **Community Resources:**
  Providing links to forums and documentation helps foster a collaborative environment.

Benefits of Open Source and Collaborative Innovation

Aspect	Benefits
Accelerated Development	Faster innovation through shared knowledge and resources.
Transparency	Builds trust and improves security through open peer review.
Customization	Enables tailored solutions to meet specific organizational needs.
Community Support	Fosters continuous improvement through collective problem-solving.

Evolving architectures and adaptive systems are at the forefront of the next wave of innovation in autonomous multi-agent systems. As challenges grow more complex, future systems will need to be modular, decentralized, and self-adaptive, capable of integrating advanced AI, IoT, and emerging technologies. Open source and collaborative innovation play a crucial role in this evolution by accelerating development, promoting transparency, and enabling customization through community-driven efforts.

By embracing these future trends, LangGraph will continue to empower developers and organizations to build robust, scalable, and intelligent systems that can adapt to the rapidly changing technological landscape. Through collaborative efforts and a commitment to innovation, the future of autonomous systems holds the promise of unprecedented advancements and transformative impacts across industries.

14.5: Preparing for the Next Wave of Technological Change

Strategic Insights for Long-Term Success

As technology continues to evolve at a rapid pace, organizations and developers must proactively prepare for the next wave of innovation. The long-term success of autonomous multi-agent systems, such as those built with LangGraph, depends not only on current capabilities but also on the ability to adapt, evolve, and integrate emerging technologies. This chapter provides strategic insights to help you future-proof your systems and position your organization for sustained success.

---

1. Understanding the Evolving Technological Landscape

Embracing Continuous Change

- **Rapid Innovation:**
  New technologies such as advanced AI, quantum computing, edge computing, and enhanced IoT devices are emerging at an unprecedented rate. Staying informed about these developments is crucial.
- **Market Dynamics:**
  As industries become increasingly digitized, the competitive landscape shifts. Organizations must anticipate changes in consumer behavior, regulatory environments, and technological capabilities.

Key Trends Impacting Autonomous Systems

- **Advanced AI and ML Integration:**
  Deep learning, reinforcement learning, and federated learning will continue to enhance decision-making, enabling agents to learn and adapt in real time.
- **Edge Computing and IoT Expansion:**
  The proliferation of high-precision sensors, faster networks (e.g., 5G

and beyond), and edge computing will facilitate real-time data processing and reduced latency.

- **Decentralized and Secure Architectures:**
  Technologies such as blockchain and distributed ledger systems will further secure decentralized agent interactions and ensure data integrity.
- **Sustainable Technologies:**
  Energy-efficient computing and green IT practices will become increasingly important, both from a cost and environmental perspective.

2. Strategic Planning for Future-Proofing

Develop a Forward-Looking Roadmap

- **Long-Term Vision:**
  Establish a clear, long-term vision that aligns with emerging trends and market needs. Consider how new technologies can be integrated into your existing framework and identify areas where innovation can create a competitive advantage.
- **Milestone Setting:**
  Define short-, medium-, and long-term milestones. These should include goals for integrating emerging technologies, improving system performance, and expanding functional capabilities.
- **Flexibility and Modularity:**
  Design your system architecture to be modular and loosely coupled. This approach facilitates easier upgrades, component replacements, and integration with new technologies without overhauling the entire system.

Example Roadmap Table

Timeframe	Strategic Focus	Key Actions	Expected Outcome
Short Term (0-6 months)	Assess and Optimize Current Infrastructure	Conduct comprehensive system audits; implement performance tuning and automated monitoring.	Improved efficiency; identification of bottlenecks.

Timeframe	Strategic Focus	Key Actions	Expected Outcome
Medium Term (6-12 months)	Integrate Emerging Technologies	Pilot projects with advanced ML models, federated learning, and edge computing modules.	Enhanced decision-making; reduced latency; scalable architecture.
Long Term (12-24 months)	Transition to a Fully Adaptive and Decentralized System	Deploy decentralized coordination mechanisms; adopt blockchain for secure agent interactions; evolve system modularity for future integration.	Future-proof, resilient, and agile multi-agent systems.

3. Investing in Innovation and Agility

Cultivate a Culture of Continuous Improvement

- **Agile Methodologies:**
  Adopt agile practices that emphasize iterative development, frequent releases, and constant feedback. Agile methodologies enable rapid response to market changes and emerging technologies.
- **Research and Development (R&D):**
  Invest in R&D to experiment with and integrate next-generation technologies. Encourage pilot projects, hackathons, and innovation labs where developers can explore new ideas without impacting production systems.
- **Training and Upskilling:**
  Regularly train teams on emerging trends and new tools. Foster an environment where continuous learning is a core value, ensuring that your workforce remains skilled and adaptable.

Open Innovation and Collaboration

- **Community Engagement:**
  Actively participate in open source communities, attend conferences, and collaborate with industry consortia. Open source projects, like LangGraph, thrive on community contributions and shared expertise.

- **Partnerships:**
  Form strategic partnerships with technology providers, academic institutions, and startups to leverage external innovation and gain early access to cutting-edge technologies.
- **Innovation Ecosystem:**
  Create platforms and forums where internal and external stakeholders can share insights, collaborate on projects, and contribute to the evolution of the system.

4. Leveraging Metrics for Continuous Adaptation

Define and Monitor Key Performance Indicators (KPIs)

- **Performance Metrics:**
  Track system metrics such as response time, throughput, error rates, and resource utilization. Use these KPIs to guide continuous improvement efforts.
- **Innovation Metrics:**
  Measure the impact of new technology integrations by tracking improvements in decision accuracy, latency reduction, and scalability enhancements.
- **Feedback Mechanisms:**
  Implement feedback loops with end-users and stakeholders to ensure that system updates align with user needs and industry demands.

Tools for Ongoing Monitoring and Analysis

- **Real-Time Dashboards:**
  Utilize monitoring tools like Prometheus and Grafana to visualize system performance and quickly identify deviations from expected performance.
- **Automated Alerts:**
  Set up threshold-based alerts to notify your team when critical metrics indicate potential issues, enabling proactive adjustments.
- **Regular Review Meetings:**
  Establish a routine for performance review and strategic planning sessions, where data is analyzed, insights are shared, and next steps are determined.

Preparing for the next wave of technological change requires a strategic, proactive approach. As emerging technologies continue to reshape the landscape of autonomous systems, it is essential to adopt a forward-looking mindset, invest in continuous innovation, and maintain a culture of agility and learning.

By developing a detailed roadmap, embracing modular and decentralized architectures, and fostering community collaboration through open source initiatives, organizations can ensure long-term success and resilience. Continuous monitoring, performance tuning, and agile development practices will further enable systems to adapt to new challenges, ensuring that your LangGraph-based multi-agent systems remain at the cutting edge of technological innovation.

Through these strategic insights and best practices, you are well-equipped to navigate the evolving technological landscape and drive sustained success in the era of advanced autonomous systems.

Chapter 15: Appendices and Resources

This chapter provides essential reference materials to help you set up and use LangGraph effectively. It includes a detailed installation and environment setup guide, as well as an API reference and command cheat sheet for quick lookups of frequently used commands and endpoints. These resources are designed to be comprehensive, ensuring that both new and experienced users can quickly get up to speed and maintain their systems with ease.

15.1 LangGraph Installation and Environment Setup (Detailed Guide)

This section provides step-by-step instructions for installing LangGraph and configuring your development environment. It also includes troubleshooting tips to help you overcome common issues that may arise during setup.

Prerequisites

Before installing LangGraph, ensure that your system meets the following requirements:

Component	Minimum Requirement	Recommended
Operating System	Windows 10, macOS 10.13+, or Linux (any modern distro)	Latest version of your preferred OS
Processor	Dual-core CPU	Quad-core or higher
Memory (RAM)	4 GB	8 GB or more
Disk Space	At least 500 MB available	1 GB or more for development tools and libraries
Python Version	Python 3.8	Python 3.9 or later
Internet Connection	Required for downloading packages	Stable high-speed connection for smoother installations

Step-by-Step Installation Instructions

Follow these steps to install LangGraph on your system:

1. Install Python

- **Download Python:**
  - o Visit the <u>official Python website</u> and download Python 3.8 or a later version.
- **Installation:**
  - o Follow the installation instructions for your operating system.
- **Verify Installation:**
  - o Open your terminal (or Command Prompt on Windows) and run:

  bash

  python --version

  - o You should see output similar to:

  nginx

  Python 3.9.7

2. Set Up a Virtual Environment

Creating a virtual environment is a best practice that isolates your project's dependencies from the global Python environment.

- **Create a Virtual Environment:**

  bash

  python -m venv env

- **Activate the Virtual Environment:**
  - o **Windows:**

  bash

  .\env\Scripts\activate

  - o **macOS/Linux:**

bash

source env/bin/activate

- **Verify Activation:**
  - o Your terminal prompt should now include the environment name (e.g., (env)).

3. Install LangGraph

With your virtual environment activated, install LangGraph using pip:

bash

pip install langgraph

- **Verify Installation:**
  - o Run the following command to confirm that LangGraph is installed:

    bash

    python -c "import langgraph; print('LangGraph installed successfully!')"

4. Configure Your Development Environment

To streamline your workflow, configure your preferred Integrated Development Environment (IDE):

- **Recommended IDEs:**
  - o Visual Studio Code
  - o PyCharm
- **Configure the Python Interpreter:**
  - o Ensure your IDE is set to use the virtual environment's interpreter. In VS Code, for example, open the Command Palette (Ctrl+Shift+P or Cmd+Shift+P on macOS), type "Python: Select Interpreter," and choose the interpreter from your env folder.
- **Additional Tools:**
  - o Consider installing code linters (e.g., flake8, pylint) and formatters (e.g., black) to maintain code quality:

bash

pip install flake8 pylint black

Troubleshooting Common Installation Issues

Issue	Possible Cause	Solution
Python not recognized	Python installation path not added to system PATH	Add Python to your PATH or specify the full path during installation.
Virtual environment activation failure	Incorrect activation command or missing scripts	Double-check your OS-specific activation command; ensure the env folder exists.
Dependency conflicts during installation	Conflicting versions of packages installed globally	Use a virtual environment to isolate dependencies; consider upgrading pip (pip install --upgrade pip).
LangGraph import error	Incomplete or failed installation	Verify installation with pip list; reinstall LangGraph if necessary.

15.2 API Reference and Command Cheat Sheet

This section serves as a quick reference guide to the most frequently used LangGraph commands, API endpoints, and functions. It is designed for rapid lookup, helping developers find what they need quickly without sifting through extensive documentation.

Common LangGraph API Commands

Below is a table summarizing key commands and endpoints used in LangGraph, along with their descriptions and example usage.

Command/Function	Description	Example Usage
langgraph init	Initializes a new LangGraph project in the current directory.	langgraph init my_project

Command/Function	Description	Example Usage
langgraph run	Starts the LangGraph system and runs all agents.	langgraph run
add_agent(agent_instance)	Registers a new agent with the LangGraph system.	system.add_agent(my_agent)
send_message(message, target)	Sends a message from one agent to another.	agent.send_message("Hello", target=another_agent)
subscribe(event, handler)	Subscribes an agent to a specific event type with a handler function.	system.subscribe("event_name", handler_function)
get_status()	Retrieves the current status of the LangGraph system.	status = system.get_status()
register_module(module_instance)	Registers a custom module or plugin with the LangGraph system.	system.register_module(custom_module)
update_agent(agent_instance, new_attributes)	Updates an agent's attributes.	system.update_agent(agent, {"status": "active"})

API Endpoint Reference

For developers integrating external systems or building on top of LangGraph's API, here are some common endpoints provided by the LangGraph framework:

Endpoint	HTTP Method	Description	Example Request
/api/agents	GET	Retrieve a list of all registered agents.	GET /api/agents
/api/agents/{agent_id}	GET	Retrieve details for a specific agent.	GET /api/agents/agent_1
/api/agents	POST	Register a new agent.	POST /api/agents with JSON payload { "name": "Agent1", "type": "Sensor" }
/api/messages	POST	Send a message between agents.	POST /api/messages with JSON payload { "from": "Agent1", "to": "Agent2", "message": "Hello" }
/api/status	GET	Retrieve the current system status and performance metrics.	GET /api/status

Quick Command Cheat Sheet

Below is a concise cheat sheet of frequently used LangGraph commands for rapid reference:

plaintext

```
# Initialize a new LangGraph project:
langgraph init my_project

# Run the LangGraph system:
langgraph run

# Add an agent to the system (Python API):
system.add_agent(agent_instance)

# Send a message from one agent to another (Python API):
```

```python
agent.send_message("Your message", target=another_agent)

# Subscribe to an event (Python API):
system.subscribe("event_name", handler_function)

# Update an agent's attributes:
system.update_agent(agent_instance, {"status": "active"})

# Retrieve system status:
status = system.get_status()
print(status)
```

Example: Using the API in a Python Script

Below is a sample Python script demonstrating the use of LangGraph API functions to initialize a system, add an agent, and send a message:

python

```python
# sample_usage.py

from langgraph import GraphSystem, Agent

# Define a simple agent class
class MyAgent(Agent):
    def __init__(self, name):
        super().__init__(name)

    def act(self):
        print(f"{self.name} is now active.")

    def receive_message(self, message, sender):
        print(f"{self.name} received a message from {sender.name}: {message}")

# Initialize the LangGraph system
system = GraphSystem()

# Create agent instances
agent1 = MyAgent("Agent1")
agent2 = MyAgent("Agent2")
```

```
# Add agents to the system
system.add_agent(agent1)
system.add_agent(agent2)

# Agent1 performs an action
agent1.act()

# Agent1 sends a message to Agent2
agent1.send_message("Hello, Agent2!", target=agent2)

# Retrieve and print system status
status = system.get_status()
print("System Status:", status)
```

Explanation:

- **Initialization:**
  The script initializes a LangGraph system and creates two agent instances.
- **Agent Registration:**
  Agents are added to the system using the add_agent() function.
- **Communication:**
  Agent1 sends a message to Agent2 using the send_message() method.
- **Status Retrieval:**
  The system status is retrieved and printed, demonstrating a complete workflow using LangGraph's API.

This chapter has provided a comprehensive set of appendices and reference materials to support the development and maintenance of your LangGraph-based systems. The detailed installation and environment setup guide in Section 15.1 ensures that you can set up your development environment with ease and troubleshoot common issues effectively. Meanwhile, the API reference and command cheat sheet in Section 15.2 offer quick access to essential commands and endpoints, facilitating rapid development and integration.

By using these resources, you can streamline your workflow, maintain consistency across projects, and quickly resolve issues, thereby enhancing the overall productivity and effectiveness of your autonomous multi-agent systems. Whether you are just starting out or are an experienced developer, these appendices serve as a vital toolkit for long-term success with LangGraph.

15.3 Glossary of Terms and Acronyms

Understanding the terminology used in multi-agent systems and the LangGraph framework is critical for clear communication and effective collaboration. Below is a glossary that defines key concepts and common acronyms, along with brief explanations to help you quickly grasp the fundamental ideas.

Glossary Table

Term / Acronym	Definition	Example/Explanation
Agent	An autonomous entity that perceives its environment, makes decisions, and acts upon them.	A robot in an industrial plant or a software entity executing trades in a financial system.
Multi-Agent System (MAS)	A system composed of multiple interacting agents that work together to achieve common or individual goals.	A network of drones coordinating to survey an area or autonomous vehicles communicating to manage traffic flow.
LangGraph	A framework for building and managing autonomous multi-agent systems using graph-based models.	It represents agents as nodes and their interactions as edges, simplifying system design and visualization.
Node	The fundamental unit in a graph representing an entity, such as an agent, device, or data point.	In LangGraph, each autonomous agent is typically represented as a node in the graph.
Edge	The connection between two nodes in a graph, representing the relationship or	An edge can indicate that two sensors are exchanging data or that

Term / Acronym	Definition	Example/Explanation
	communication between agents.	two agents are collaborating on a task.
API (Application Programming Interface)	A set of rules and protocols for building and interacting with software applications.	LangGraph provides APIs to create, manage, and monitor agents.
CI/CD (Continuous Integration/Continuous Deployment)	A development practice where code changes are automatically tested, integrated, and deployed to production.	Tools like Jenkins and GitHub Actions facilitate CI/CD pipelines for LangGraph projects.
Docker	A platform for containerizing applications, allowing them to run consistently across different environments.	LangGraph applications can be containerized using Docker for easy deployment.
Kubernetes	An open-source platform for automating deployment, scaling, and managing containerized applications.	Kubernetes orchestrates Docker containers to ensure high availability and scalability of LangGraph agents.
Edge Computing	A distributed computing paradigm that brings computation and data storage closer to the sources of data, reducing latency.	In IoT applications, data is processed on devices at the edge rather than sending it to a centralized cloud server.
Federated Learning	A machine learning technique that trains an algorithm across multiple decentralized devices holding local data samples, without exchanging them.	Useful in healthcare applications where data privacy is critical.
Reinforcement Learning (RL)	A type of machine learning where agents	RL enables agents to optimize their behavior

Term / Acronym	Definition	Example/Explanation
	learn to make decisions by performing actions and receiving feedback in the form of rewards or penalties.	through trial and error in dynamic environments.
Blockchain	A decentralized, distributed ledger technology that records transactions across many computers so that the record cannot be altered retroactively.	Can be used in multi-agent systems to ensure secure and transparent communication among agents.
Prometheus	An open-source systems monitoring and alerting toolkit designed for reliability and scalability.	Often used with Grafana to monitor system performance metrics in real-time.
Grafana	An open-source platform for monitoring and observability that provides dashboards for data visualization.	Grafana visualizes metrics collected by Prometheus, such as CPU usage and network latency.
ELK Stack	A collection of three open-source products: Elasticsearch, Logstash, and Kibana, used for log aggregation and analysis.	Helps in centralized logging and troubleshooting of distributed systems.
Asynchronous Programming	A programming paradigm that allows for non-blocking operations, enabling the execution of multiple tasks concurrently.	Python's asyncio library supports asynchronous programming to improve system responsiveness.
Load Balancing	The process of distributing workloads evenly across multiple agents or servers to	Round-robin scheduling is a common load balancing technique in distributed systems.

Term / Acronym	Definition	Example/Explanation
	optimize resource utilization and minimize response time.	
Failover	A backup operational mode in which the functions of a system component (such as an agent) are assumed by secondary systems when the primary system fails.	Ensures high availability in multi-agent systems by automatically switching to redundant components during a failure.
CI/CD	See Continuous Integration/Continuous Deployment.	
ML (Machine Learning)	A subset of artificial intelligence focused on the development of algorithms that can learn from and make predictions on data.	Utilized in LangGraph to enable autonomous agents to improve decision-making through data analysis.

How to Use the Glossary

- **Quick Lookup:**
  Refer to this glossary whenever you encounter unfamiliar terminology in LangGraph documentation, code, or discussions with team members.
- **Educational Resource:**
  New team members and stakeholders can use this glossary to build a foundational understanding of the key concepts and technologies that underpin autonomous multi-agent systems.
- **Consistent Communication:**
  A shared vocabulary helps ensure that everyone on the project is aligned and can communicate effectively about system design and troubleshooting.

15.4 Additional Resources and Further Reading

Staying informed about the latest developments and best practices in autonomous systems, multi-agent frameworks, and related technologies is essential for long-term success. This section provides a curated list of books, articles, online communities, and official documentation to help you deepen your understanding and keep up with industry trends.

Books

1. **"Multi-Agent Systems: Algorithmic, Game-Theoretic, and Logical Foundations"** by Yoav Shoham and Kevin Leyton-Brown
   o **Description:**
   This comprehensive text covers the theoretical foundations of multi-agent systems, including algorithms, game theory, and logic.
   o **Benefits:**
   Provides a deep theoretical understanding that can inform practical implementations in LangGraph.
2. **"Reinforcement Learning: An Introduction"** by Richard S. Sutton and Andrew G. Barto
   o **Description:**
   A foundational book on reinforcement learning that explains key concepts and algorithms.
   o **Benefits:**
   Essential reading for integrating RL into autonomous agent decision-making.
3. **"Designing Data-Intensive Applications"** by Martin Kleppmann
   o **Description:**
   Explores modern data architectures and systems, focusing on scalability, reliability, and maintainability.
   o **Benefits:**
   Offers valuable insights into building scalable distributed systems, relevant to LangGraph deployments.

Articles and Research Papers

1. **"A Survey of Multi-Agent Reinforcement Learning"**
   o **Description:**
   Provides an overview of current trends, challenges, and techniques in multi-agent reinforcement learning.

- o **Benefits:**
  Helpful for understanding advanced AI integration in LangGraph.
2. **"Edge Computing: Vision and Challenges"**
   - o **Description:**
     Discusses the potential and challenges of edge computing, a key trend in IoT and autonomous systems.
   - o **Benefits:**
     Useful for designing systems that require low-latency, distributed data processing.
3. **"Blockchain for Decentralized Trust in Autonomous Systems"**
   - o **Description:**
     Explores how blockchain technology can secure and enhance the trustworthiness of distributed systems.
   - o **Benefits:**
     Relevant for ensuring data integrity and security in multi-agent architectures.

Online Communities and Forums

1. **GitHub Repositories:**
   - o **LangGraph Official Repository:**
     Engage with the community, report issues, and contribute code.
   - o **Open Source Projects in Multi-Agent Systems:**
     Explore related projects and gain insights from community-contributed solutions.
2. **Stack Overflow:**
   - o **Description:**
     A question-and-answer platform where you can ask for help, share knowledge, and find solutions related to LangGraph and multi-agent systems.
   - o **Benefits:**
     Access to a vast community of developers and experts.
3. **Reddit Communities:**
   - o **Subreddits:**
     - r/MachineLearning
     - r/ArtificialIntelligence
     - r/IOT
   - o **Benefits:**
     Engage in discussions, share articles, and stay updated on the latest trends.

4. **Slack and Discord Channels:**
   o **Description:**
     Join channels dedicated to AI, ML, IoT, and multi-agent systems for real-time discussions and networking.
   o **Benefits:**
     Immediate support, collaboration opportunities, and a platform for sharing ideas.

Documentation and Official Resources

1. **LangGraph Official Documentation:**
   o **Description:**
     The official documentation provides detailed guides, API references, tutorials, and troubleshooting tips.
   o **Benefits:**
     Primary source for understanding and effectively using the LangGraph framework.
2. **Python Documentation:**
   o **Description:**
     Comprehensive resources for Python programming, including libraries and modules used in LangGraph.
   o **Benefits:**
     Essential for debugging, extending, and optimizing your code.
3. **Kubernetes and Docker Documentation:**
   o **Description:**
     Official guides and tutorials for containerization and orchestration, crucial for deploying LangGraph in cloud environments.
   o **Benefits:**
     Helps you understand best practices for deploying and scaling containerized applications.

How to Use Additional Resources

- **Continuous Learning:**
  Regularly read books, research papers, and articles to stay informed about emerging trends and technologies.
- **Engage with the Community:**
  Participate in online forums and community discussions to share experiences, ask questions, and learn from others.
- **Experiment and Contribute:**
  Explore open source projects on GitHub and consider contributing to

LangGraph or related projects to enhance your skills and influence the community.

The glossary and additional resources provided in this chapter are designed to serve as comprehensive reference materials for anyone working with LangGraph and autonomous multi-agent systems. The glossary clarifies key concepts and terminology, ensuring a common understanding among developers, stakeholders, and users. Meanwhile, the curated list of books, articles, online communities, and official documentation offers a pathway for continuous learning and growth.

By leveraging these resources, you can deepen your knowledge, stay updated on emerging trends, and contribute to the vibrant community driving innovation in autonomous systems. Whether you are a beginner or an experienced practitioner, these appendices are invaluable tools to support your long-term success and advancement in the field.

Index

The index provided below is a comprehensive, alphabetical listing of key topics, terms, and acronyms covered throughout this guide on LangGraph and autonomous multi-agent systems. This index is designed to serve as a quick reference to help you locate discussions, code examples, and detailed explanations within the text. Each entry includes brief pointers to the sections or chapters where the topics are discussed.

A

- **Access Control**
  See also: Authentication, RBAC
    - Discussion in Chapter 11.5 (Security, Compliance, and Maintenance in the Cloud)
- **Agent**
    - Definition and characteristics in Chapter 3 (Fundamentals of Autonomous Multi-Agent Systems)
    - Implementation examples in Chapters 7 (Implementing Autonomous Agents) and 12 (Practical Applications)
- **Agent Communication**

- o Explored in Chapter 3.3 (Communication Protocols in Multi-Agent Systems)
  - o Asynchronous and message-passing methods in Chapters 7 and 10
- **Agent Development Lifecycle**
  - o Detailed in Chapter 7.1 (Implementing Autonomous Agents in LangGraph)

B

- **Batching**
  - o Technique for reducing communication overhead discussed in Chapter 10.3 (Load Balancing and Concurrency Management)
- **Blockchain**
  - o Role in decentralized trust highlighted in Chapter 14.1 (Emerging Technologies in Autonomous Systems)
  - o Mentioned in discussions about evolving architectures in Chapter 14.3

C

- **CI/CD (Continuous Integration/Continuous Deployment)**
  - o Concepts and tools covered in Chapter 11.4 (CI/CD and Automated Deployment Pipelines)
- **Centralized Architecture**
  - o Characteristics and trade-offs discussed in Chapter 6.3 (Architectural Patterns for Multi-Agent Systems)
- **Code Optimization**
  - o Profiling techniques and algorithm improvements outlined in Chapter 10 (Performance Optimization Techniques)
- **Containerization**
  - o Docker usage and benefits detailed in Chapter 11.2 (Containerization and Orchestration)
- **Continuous Monitoring**
  - o Best practices discussed in Chapter 10.5 (Performance Tuning and Ongoing Monitoring) and Chapter 13 (Troubleshooting and Maintenance)

D

- **Data Caching**
    - Strategies for reducing redundant computations in Chapter 10.4 (Resource Management and Memory Optimization)
- **Decentralized Architecture**
    - Detailed in Chapter 6.3 (Architectural Patterns for Multi-Agent Systems) and revisited in Chapter 14.1 (Emerging Technologies)
- **Distributed Systems**
    - General concepts and challenges explained across Chapters 9 (Scalability) and 11 (Cloud Deployment)

E

- **Edge Computing**
    - Benefits for reducing latency and enabling local processing in Chapter 14.1 (Emerging Technologies in Autonomous Systems)
- **ELK Stack**
    - Use for centralized logging and troubleshooting discussed in Chapters 10.5 and 13 (Ongoing Monitoring and Debugging)

F

- **Federated Learning**
    - Introduced as a privacy-preserving ML technique in Chapter 14.1 (Emerging Technologies in Autonomous Systems)

G

- **Grafana**

- o Tools for visualization of metrics, referenced in Chapter 10.5 (Ongoing Monitoring) and Chapter 11.5 (Security, Compliance, and Maintenance in the Cloud)
- **Graph Models**
  - o Fundamental concepts in Chapter 4 (Graph Theory Essentials)
  - o Customization strategies in Chapter 8 (Advanced LangGraph Techniques and Patterns)
- **Graph Traversal**
  - o Techniques (BFS, DFS, A*) detailed in Chapter 4.3 (Graph Traversal and Search Algorithms)

H

- **Healthcare**
  - o Applications and use cases in personalized medicine discussed in Chapter 12.4 (Healthcare and Personalized Medicine)
- **High Availability**
  - o Strategies and best practices for fault tolerance in Chapter 9 (Scalability) and Chapter 11.5 (Security, Compliance, and Maintenance in the Cloud)

I

- **In-Memory Graphs**
  - o Storage strategies discussed in Chapter 4.4 (Data Structures and Storage Strategies)
- **Interoperability**
  - o The need for standardized protocols emphasized in Chapter 14.1 (Emerging Technologies) and Chapter 11 (Cloud Deployment)

K

- **Kubernetes**

- Orchestration platform details in Chapter 11.2 (Containerization and Orchestration)

L

- **LangGraph**
  - Overview and architecture detailed in Chapter 1 (Overview of LangGraph and Autonomous Systems) and Chapter 5 (Inside the LangGraph Architecture)
- **Load Balancing**
  - Techniques and strategies for even workload distribution explained in Chapter 10.3 (Load Balancing and Concurrency Management)
- **Logging**
  - Best practices and tools for effective logging discussed in Chapters 13 (Troubleshooting and Maintenance) and 10.5 (Ongoing Monitoring)

M

- **Machine Learning (ML)**
  - Applications in predictive analytics and decision-making described in Chapters 8.3 (Complex Decision-Making and AI Integration) and 14.1 (Emerging Technologies in Autonomous Systems)
- **Microservices**
  - Architectural style discussed in Chapter 11.2 (Containerization and Orchestration) and Chapter 14.1 (Emerging Technologies)
- **Multi-Agent System (MAS)**
  - Definition and foundational concepts in Chapter 3 (Fundamentals of Autonomous Multi-Agent Systems)

N

- **Node**

- Basic unit of graph theory explained in Chapter 4.1 (Basic Concepts in Graph Theory)

O

- **Open Source**
  - The role of community and collaborative innovation described in Chapter 14.4 (The Role of Open Source and Collaborative Innovation)
- **Optimization**
  - Performance and resource optimization techniques detailed in Chapters 10 (Performance Optimization Techniques) and 13 (Troubleshooting and Maintenance)

P

- **Performance Tuning**
  - Strategies for maintaining system health outlined in Chapters 10.5 (Performance Tuning and Ongoing Monitoring) and 13.5 (Performance Tuning and Ongoing Monitoring)
- **Profiling**
  - Tools and methodologies for performance measurement discussed in Chapter 10.1 (Profiling and Benchmarking Your System)
- **Prometheus**
  - Monitoring tool described in Chapter 10.5 (Ongoing Monitoring)

Q

- **Quantum Computing**
  - Emerging technology discussed in Chapter 14.1 (Emerging Technologies in Autonomous Systems)

R

- **Real-Time Monitoring**
  - Continuous monitoring practices explained in Chapter 10.5 (Performance Tuning and Ongoing Monitoring)
- **Reinforcement Learning (RL)**
  - Advanced ML technique outlined in Chapter 14.1 (Emerging Technologies in Autonomous Systems)
- **Resource Management**
  - Strategies for efficient resource use discussed in Chapter 10.4 (Resource Management and Memory Optimization)
- **RBAC (Role-Based Access Control)**
  - Security mechanism mentioned in Chapter 11.5 (Security, Compliance, and Maintenance in the Cloud)

S

- **Scalability**
  - Challenges and solutions discussed extensively in Chapter 9 (Principles of Scalability in Multi-Agent Systems)
- **Security**
  - Best practices for data protection and regulatory adherence covered in Chapter 11.5 (Security, Compliance, and Maintenance in the Cloud)
- **Self-Adaptive Systems**
  - Concepts of self-healing and adaptive architectures detailed in Chapter 14.3 (Evolving Architectures and Adaptive Systems)
- **Smart Cities**
  - Applications in urban planning and resource management described in Chapter 12.3 (Smart Cities and Infrastructure Management)
- **Simulation**
  - Tools and methodologies for simulating agent behavior discussed in Chapters 7 (Implementing Autonomous Agents) and 10 (Performance Optimization Techniques)

T

- **Troubleshooting**
  - Techniques for problem isolation and debugging explained in Chapter 13 (Troubleshooting and Maintenance)
- **Tuning**
  - Performance tuning strategies detailed in Chapters 10 (Performance Optimization Techniques) and 13 (Troubleshooting and Maintenance)

U

- **Uptime**
  - Metrics for system availability discussed in Chapters 9 (Scalability) and 11 (Cloud Deployment)

V

- **Virtual Machines (VMs)**
  - Cloud compute resources discussed in Chapter 11.1 (Overview of Cloud Platforms and Services)
- **VPC (Virtual Private Cloud)**
  - Network isolation concepts described in Chapter 11.1 (Overview of Cloud Platforms and Services)

W

- **Workload Distribution**
  - Load balancing and scheduling strategies outlined in Chapter 10.3 (Load Balancing and Concurrency Management)

How to Use This Index

- **Quick Navigation:**
  Use the index to quickly locate topics of interest by scanning the alphabetical list of terms.

- **Reference Guide:**
  Refer back to specific chapters or sections where these topics are discussed in detail.
- **Learning and Review:**
  The index serves as a learning aid, reinforcing key concepts and helping you review essential terminology.

Conclusion

As we draw this comprehensive guide to a close, I hope that you feel both enlightened and inspired by the transformative potential of LangGraph and its applications in autonomous multi-agent systems. Throughout this book, I've taken you on an in-depth journey—from foundational concepts in graph theory and the design of autonomous agents to advanced techniques in performance optimization, cloud deployment, and real-world applications across smart cities, healthcare, finance, and more.

You've seen how LangGraph empowers you to build robust, scalable, and adaptive systems that can respond dynamically to ever-changing environments. The detailed code examples, practical case studies, and clear, step-by-step instructions are all designed to give you the tools and confidence to innovate in your own projects. Whether you're fine-tuning agent interactions to reduce latency or integrating cutting-edge AI and IoT technologies, this guide provides both the theory and the actionable insights needed to excel.

What makes this book truly unique is its commitment to not only explaining the "how" but also the "why" behind each concept, ensuring that you understand the strategic value of every best practice and architectural pattern discussed. This is more than just a technical manual—it's a roadmap for the future of autonomous systems, a vision of where technology is headed, and a call to action for developers, researchers, and innovators alike.

We believe that the future of technology is collaborative and ever-evolving. With LangGraph, you're not just adopting a tool; you're joining a community that is pushing the boundaries of what's possible. As you apply these concepts to your projects, we invite you to share your successes, contribute your ideas, and engage with others who are equally passionate about autonomous systems.

We hope that after reading this book, you'll be motivated to dive back in—exploring new sections, revisiting complex topics, and perhaps even experimenting with your own innovative implementations. Your feedback is invaluable, and we encourage you to leave a review, share your thoughts, and discuss your experiences with peers and in community forums.

Thank you for embarking on this journey with us. Here's to building smarter, more adaptive, and truly revolutionary systems that will shape the future of technology. Enjoy the exploration, and let your ideas spark conversations that drive the next wave of innovation!